The Road Ahead

Other Books by JOHN T. FLYNN

The Road Ahead

AMERICA'S CREEPING REVOLUTION

John T. Flynn

1949

THE DEVIN-ADAIR COMPANY

New York

Contents

"If we could first know where we are and whither we are tending, we could better judge what to do, and how to do it."

Abraham Lincoln, at Springfield, Ill., June 16, 1858

"For as in the days that were before the flood they were eating and drinking, marrying and giving in marriage, until the day that Noah entered into the ark.

"And knew not until the flood came and took them all away."

Matthew, Ch. 24, Verses 38, 39.

CHAPTER ONE

Our Real Enemy

My purpose in writing this book is to attempt to describe the road along which this country is traveling to its destruction.

Human societies come under the influence of great tides of thought and appetite that run unseen deeply below the surface of society. After a while these powerful streams of opinion and desire move the whole social mass along with them without the individuals in the mass being aware of the direction in which they are going. Up to a certain point it is possible to resist these controlling tides and to reverse them, but a time comes when they are so strong that society loses its power of decision over the direction in which it is going.

I believe we are now moving along under the dominion of such tides and that all the things we do to deal with our accumulating perils are futile because we do not understand the tides nor the direction in which they are carrying us. I believe that we still have in our hands the means of checking this onrush to disaster. We still may consciously control our destiny. But I feel sure that we are moving toward a crisis which will be for us the moment of decision. It will be at that point we will either use or lose our final opportunity to determine the direction along which this nation will travel.

For a while, as the war came to an end, our people were nervous about what was supposed to be the reconversion problem and the inevitable deflation. At the end of a year there was no sign of the crisis. Despite solemn predictions in the second year, the crisis did not come, nor in the third nor fourth year after peace was concluded. Even business men began to wonder about this. Can it be that this new thing works? Maybe, they thought, there will be no crisis. This feeling had settled fairly

7

snugly into the plans and hopes of almost every class. Our economic system had been altered—and our political system as well. Of course the explanation of this continuing war boom was quite obvious. The hot war had ended and the cold war had been launched. Having lost Japan and Germany as enemies, we managed to acquire a new one—Russia. And so, instead of ending our vast war expenditures wholly, we continued to spend billions a year on our military establishments, plus more billions to reconstruct Europe and save her from being engulfed by the Communist terror.

Obviously we cannot go on the way we are now traveling. We do have a very large number of people employed, though unemployment has risen to 4,000,000 workers and the number continues to increase with each month. This employment, under the present system, is made possible by what is called the cold war. We are spending 15 billion dollars on our defenses because of the threat of war with Russia. We are spending about five billion more to rehabilitate Europe—spending the money in our factories and on our farms to send supplies abroad. We now propose to spend another 1.5 billion to rearm Europe. But suppose the cold war were to come to an end? We cannot seriously contemplate keeping it up forever. Suppose we had to cut our military outlays to a peacetime basis and make an end of attempting to support and arm western Europe. This would immediately result in throwing at least four million people out of work in the first place and at least four or five million more when the first four million quit buying at the stores. In short, our economic system is now a "war" economy—a "cold war" economy. If the cold war should end without becoming a hot war, what then would we do?

Of course it is now beginning to seep into the minds of our people that we could have an economic crisis here even before this cold war ends. In any case, the cold war has had one significant effect. It has forced us to look at Russia for what she is and not as she was pictured to us when she was "our noble ally." And this has forced us to turn our attention to our American Communist movement. We have, as a consequence, been making war on the Communists. This has had one very serious by-product. It has dramatized the American Communist Party and its dupes as the chief internal enemy of our economic system and our form of government. And it is widely feared that a crisis here would present our native Communists with their great opportunity.

This I hold to be a mistake of the first magnitude. I insist that if every Communist in America were rounded up and liquidated, the great menace to our form of social organization would be still among us. I do not mean to underestimate the danger from the Communists. They are interested at the moment in serving the purposes of the great enemy of the whole western world—Russia. They are a traitorous bloc in our midst and they have frightening potentialities for harm in our foreign relations. But they are not as dangerous to us in the struggle now under way to change our internal institutions as another wholly indigenous movement. The leaders of this movement now actually seek to outdo us in berating the Communists with whom they were marching together but two or three years ago. They are more dangerous because they are more numerous and more respectable and they are not tainted with the odium of treachery. They are more dangerous because, as a matter of fact, they are now occupying positions of great power, have in their hands immense sections of our political machinery and are actually hailed as our brothers in the battle against the Reds. Every day that passes reduces the power of the Communists to mislead us or to promote their program among us. But every day that passes enlarges the opportunities of our real internal enemies to confuse us, to arouse us and to entice us to travel the dark road that has led every country in Europe to its doom. Acting under false colors and a name designed to conceal their real purpose and using words chosen to deceive, they are now well advanced in a sneak attack upon our whole way of life.

Our people, despite our international wars, have been so far removed from the European scene that they have not observed very closely the play of forces which in the last 30 years has been eating away the foundations of European civilization. It is very difficult for us to credit the influence which certain human appetites and frustrations and hatreds can exercise upon the mass mind of a whole nation. Our history had been, up to 20 years ago, one of almost continuous advance. We have encountered difficulties but we have managed somehow to struggle or blunder our way out of them. We have no talent as a people for pessimism. In prosperity we convinced ourselves it would last forever. When the depression came we were always sure recovery was just ahead. No one could convince us we would ever go into another European war. When the war came we were quite sure it would end swiftly and when the enemy surrendered we fondly imagined peace would attend us as a matter of course. And now, after four years of the mess which we call the "cold war" we persist in our confidence that somehow some friendly deity will save us from drifting into that kind of social disorder which has engulfed all of Europe.

Yet while we cherish this fatuous dream the same forces that ruined Germany and Italy and France and Britain are mobilizing to repeat their work of destruction upon us. The germs of that fatal sickness—the sickness of the twentieth century which has circled the western world—are already fastened in the very vitals of our economic and political organisms. And we can no longer refuse to recognize them.

Most of the countries in Europe have moved into the Socialist camp. The two which concern us most are Russia and Great Britain. Each has moved into socialism by a different route. Each has organized its Socialist society upon a different model. But both are Socialist. Russia was conquered overnight by a sudden, violent revolutionary convulsion. Great Britain managed its revolution upon a peaceful and gradualist pattern. It moved into socialism a little at a time. The journey took almost 40 years.

We are following, not in the footsteps of Russia, but in the footsteps of England. We are being drawn into socialism on the British gradualist model. We are well on the road—much further along than our people suspect. And if we do not clearly recognize that fact and abandon that fatal route, we will inevitably, perhaps in less than a decade, arrive at that state of socialization now before us in England. Not until we recognize this fact and all its implications will we be able to recognize "where we are and whither we are tending." Not until then will we be able to judge "what to do, and how to do it."

In England we have a perfect case history of the infection and progress of the Socialist disease—for despite the glowing terms in which its apostles promote it, socialism is a disease which fastens itself upon the body of a weakened society. This book is about America, but I must ask the reader to pause for a moment and go with me through a brief inspection of the rise of socialism in England and its swift conquest of that great nation. England was a free society more nearly resembling our own than any other European country and, until recently, the richest and most powerful nation in the world. What has happened there is far more informative for us than the story of the onset of socialism in any other country.

The Socialist government in Britain did not come into power by accident. It arrived in power in England as the result of a plan—a carefully concerted plan, laid down with great intelligence many years ago. In the next chapter I propose to describe for you step by step the unfolding of the British plan by which that once great country—the home of modern capitalism and modern free government—was led stealthily, with the aid of two "victorious" wars, to her present state.

We must see this English experiment clearly because the plan by which England was sneaked into socialism is now being promoted in this country by a coalition of politicians and revolutionary crusaders who are the counterpart of the British Fabian Socialists. It is being carried out with startling fidelity and promptness with the aid of the ignorance of the American business man and politician. And it is a grave question whether or not the program has been already so far advanced that reversal may be impossible. But this much is certain—it must be reversed and that at once or we will find ourselves trapped in a Socialist

*system in a far shorter time than was required to conquer
England.*

Let us now see by what carefully arranged stages this great
job was done upon the English people in order that we may understand better what is happening here.

CHAPTER TWO

The Fabian Dream

For a thousand years, says Winston Churchill in his war memoirs, no alien enemy has been able to invade the shores of England. It is quite true that the doughty Briton has been able to keep Hitler, as he kept Napoleon, from crossing his guarded channel. But for all that, Karl Marx made it. And now we shall see how it was done. Of course the British apologist for the present government in London will tell you his socialism has nothing to do with Marx. We shall deal with that later. For the moment, let us rest with the observation that no American can understand what is happening in America if he does not understand what has happened in England and how it was brought about.

In 1883 a small group of Socialists organized what they called the Fabian Society. In time it included such eminent persons as Sidney and Beatrice Webb, Annie Besant, George Bernard Shaw, Ramsay MacDonald and others. These Englishmen believed that if socialism was to be brought to England it would have to be done gradually and not by violent revolutionary means. They decided they would make the attempt through political methods. They adopted the policy of the Roman general, Quintus Fabius, who held the only way to defeat Hannibal was to avoid a general engagement and by clever withdrawals lure him to battle in small sectors and defeat him in sections. Hence they called the movement the Fabian movement. Their strategy as well as their program became known as Fabian Socialism.

Sidney Webb, their great statesman, later known as Lord Passfield, saw clearly that if socialism was to make any headway against the solid rock of British opinion it would have to do so by constitutional processes. The cause must move one step at a time, he insisted, taking care never to offend the moral sense of the masses who must be offered only so much at each stage as they would accept. This Fabian Society never had more than 4000 members. Yet it was this small group that made the whole amazing triumph of socialism possible in England. This triumph was not gained through sheer luck or accident. The Fabians early outlined a definite plan. They did not, of course, invent it out-of-hand in a session or two around a conference table. It grew in their minds a little at a time. It was probably not until around the turn of the century that they saw it clearly in all its parts. This plan may be briefly summarized as follows:

1. The first feature was the Fabian Society itself, which became the political planning machine that made the plans, was the training school for Socialist leaders, schooled speakers and writers and leaders, directed the national educational program and acted as the general staff of the movement.

2. The Fabians began by advocating not a Socialist State but a Welfare State as the prologue.

3. They resolved to offer their program in small successive sections—by means of gradualism, as it came to be known.

4. They decided against total State ownership of land and industry. They proposed State ownership of the great basic functions—credit, electric power, transportation, basic metals. The balance of the economic system would be left in private hands but operated under plans made by the State.

5. They held they must capture the mind of the working class and to that end must take over the apparatus—that is, the officialdom—of the labor unions.

6. They decided to form a political arm—a party—which later became the British Labor Party.

7. They decided to begin by cooperating with the Liberal Party, which corresponded to our Democratic Party, until their own Labor Party acquired strength enough to displace it.

8. They agreed they must penetrate and capture the instruments of public opinion and information—the writers, the churchmen and the schools.

This plan had one thing to be said for it. It succeeded. Its central aim was to bring on socialism without mentioning that odious word—to offer to the voters one small part of the Socialist machine at a time without the Socialist label on it; to smuggle socialism into the social fabric without arousing the suspicions of the masses. Whatever may be said for it, it was a sneak attack. Now let us see, briefly, how it worked.

Actually the movement did not get well under way until about 1905. Behold at that moment the majestic edifice of Great Britain—from her sea-girt citadel extending her sway over a vast empire spreading over all the continents, her navy patrolling the seven seas of which she was the mistress, her factories sending out mountains of products to every land from which in turn flowed golden streams of raw materials and money, her pound sterling the very symbol of financial stability, her might invincible, her very name a synonym for wealth and power. Edward VII sat upon his solid throne and England's ancient aristocracy ranged around it in grandeur and security at the heart of what was supposed to be the best of all possible worlds.

It was into this immense and virile organism that this small coterie of Socialist doctrinaires thrust themselves. They got in motion around 1905, the year the Liberal Party came to power under Campbell-Bannerman, Herbert Asquith and Lloyd George.

Nine years later the Labor Party had representatives in the British cabinet.

Four years after that their party was the official opposition, having pushed the old Liberal Party aside.

In five more years their leader, Ramsay MacDonald, was Prime Minister of England.

In this year 1949 a Socialist government rules supreme in England and England has become one of the Socialist nations. And of the 390 Socialist members in Parliament, 230 are members of the Fabian Society and 41 of its members are in the government. You may not approve of these gentlemen, but you cannot scoff at them.

Now let us look at the manner in which each of these several steps was accomplished.

Of course the existence of the Fabian Society was the first step, providing the movement with its general staff made up of men of great intelligence and with a deeply rooted and flaming zeal for their cause. The first direct move had come in a small way in 1893, when Keir Hardie, a member of the Fabians, formed the Independent Labor Party, although it comprised only a handful of labor delegates. This was the first move in the plan to capture the apparatus of the labor unions. The prime movers in this party were all Socialists. But they rejected the idea of calling this a Socialist Party. *They decided it would be easier to draw in the members of the labor unions if the word socialism were kept out and the organization called a Labor Party.*[1] The Independent Labor Party was ultimately abandoned and the final struggle carried on by its successor, the British Labor Party.

The first line of policy pursued was to push England in the direction of the Welfare State. As G. D. H. Cole says, while the new Party from the outset was "Socialist in its aims," it put its chief emphasis upon welfare and reform measures. These were the eight-hour day, abolition of overtime and piece work, public provision out of taxes for the sick, aged, widows and orphans, free nonsectarian education up to the universities, properly remunerated work for the unemployed. These measures they believed would bring the labor unions to their side. They felt that if they could capture the leaders and the official machinery of the unions, the membership would fall in behind them. These welfare measures made a powerful appeal to the trade unionists. "They hoped that if they could get the trade unions to collaborate with them . . . the rest of what they wanted would speedily follow," says Cole, and, as he put it,

[1] "British Working Class Politics, 1832-1914" by G. D. H. Cole, Routledge, London, 1941.

"the Socialist tail would be strong enough to wag the Trade Union dog." [2]

Events played into their hands. The British labor unions were looked upon in their early days as purely instruments for collective bargaining between employer and employee. They were not interested in altering the structure of British society and they kept scrupulously away from "the contamination of politics." The Fabians were determined to drag them into politics. And they very quickly found issues which aided in this plan. One was the famous Taff-Vale decision which said that a union could be held in damages caused by a strike. The Fabians convinced the labor leaders that this could be corrected only by a Parliament favorable to labor and that this called for political action. The unions were thus galvanized into political life and the process was not to end until they had been brought completely under the direction of Socialist leaders.

The first great battle was fought in 1905. The Liberal Party was returned to power in Parliament. In that election, Labor won 29 seats. But something equally as important happened. Labor made a deal with the Liberals, who agreed to support Labor proposals, in return for which Labor agreed to support Liberal Party measures, chiefly free trade. In constituencies where Labor was strongest, the Liberals supported Labor candidates. Where Liberals were strongest, Labor supported the Liberal candidates. Labor Party historians admit that many of the Labor candidates were elected as a result of these deals, including Ramsay MacDonald and Philip Snowden. But the chief significance of this was that while Labor had 29 of its own members in Parliament, there were twice as many Liberal members who owed their election to Labor Party support. As time passed this condition spread. Labor elected more and more Labor members and controlled more and more Liberal members, until *the Liberal Party found itself the prisoner of the Socialist Labor groups.*

After 1906, when Asquith, the Liberal leader, became Prime Minister and Lloyd George his Chancellor of the Exchequer,

[2] *Ibid.* (Italics added).

Lloyd George leaped into sudden and lurid notoriety with a succession of social welfare measures. They were much the same as the New Deal proposed here from 1933 to 1937. Lloyd George looked upon all these as purely social arrangements to aid the underprivileged people of England. But the Labor Party knew this was just the prelude to more vigorous action. These measures included the eight-hour day, workmen's compensation, old-age pensions, housing legislation, public payment of election expenses and, of course, invalidation of the Taff-Vale decision.

To Liberals and to humanitarian England all this was defensible social reform wholly consistent with Liberal principles and in no way an attack upon the British system of private ownership. But the Socialist Fabian Planners saw it in a wholly different light. And it is at this point we must be quite certain to see with clarity the pitfalls which opened before England and which now yawn before us.

The British Fabian Socialist saw early *the immense value of social reform for accustoming the citizens to looking to the State for the correction of all their ills. They saw that welfare agitation could be made the vehicle for importing Socialist ideas into the minds of the common man.* Max Beer said: "There was no reason for Socialists to wait for the revolution. *The realization of socialism had begun from the moment when the State became accessible to social reform ideas.*" [3]

Actually, many of the early British Socialists were little more than welfare reformers. They did not realize the immense implications of socialism. It is primarily an economic philosophy which deals not merely with the organization of the political state, but even more with the vast and complex producing and distributing machinery of the nation. It involves the most far-reaching changes in our whole way of life and the most extensive alterations in the structure of our government. George Bernard Shaw has said that in those early days no British Socialist, unless we except Ruskin, had done "twopennies' worth of economic thinking." They were, as another put it, "Social-

[3] "History of British Socialism" by M. Beer, Harcourt, Brace, 1921.

ists of the heart rather than the head," like so many of our well-intentioned religious Reds who do not have the faintest conception of the terrible explosive with which they are toying. Meantime, Labor was becoming more powerful in Parliament. It had 42 members by 1910. The capture of the labor union apparatus was complete. The Liberal Party was a prisoner and could move in no direction without the permission of the Labor Party.

Then came World War I. Labor was given several seats in the coalition cabinet. But three days after the war ended the Labor Party ordered its members out of the cabinet. It demanded "land for the workers," "a million good homes," "the capital levy," and government ownership of mines and railroads in order to raise miners' and railroad workers' wages. There was no talk of socialism. Lloyd George called a general election and Labor got 61 seats.

The dislocations produced by the war had proved too much for Lloyd George's leadership. Another election was called in 1922 which marked a turning point in British history. The Conservatives got 405 seats in Parliament. The Labor Party won 142. The Liberal Party got only 59. It had received a death wound. One of the great objectives of the Socialists had been almost attained—the extinction of the Liberals. But the issue of socialism was never presented. Millions voted for the Labor Party because they believed it was the friend of the workers. Many others were for the social reforms. Millions of troubled people were for pensions, relief, school lunches. Disillusioned soldiers were against things in general. The capital levy was presented as merely a form of soaking the rich.

Lloyd George, who had been the first eminent dupe, was in a dark and bitter mood. He wrote:

> Capitalism is to be arraigned before the Supreme Court of the nation, condemned, sentenced and executed by installments —Chinese fashion. . . . The British people, with their inherent political instinct, are beginning to realize that grave decisions must then be taken.

But he noted the popular misunderstanding of all this. He said:

> There is still a good deal of apathy and indifference. The average comfortable citizen is still inclined to think these Socialist schemes are so crazy as to be impossible. They cannot believe that 21,000,000 of sane people can possibly contemplate giving their sanction to such fantasies.

Then he asked:

> Can it be arrested? Nothing will be done until the danger is visible to every eye. To vary the metaphor no one will believe in the flood until it is upon us. Trained weather prophets who forecast its coming will be laughed at or told that they have a personal or party interest in ark building. It is an old tale—as old as the dawn of history. 'As in the days before the flood they were eating and drinking and knew not until the flood came and took them all away.' [4]

Here was Lloyd George, who had been out upon the seacoast 16 years earlier opening the first dikes for his Socialist allies in Parliament, now out upon the housetops warning the population against the flood. However, he was uttering a prophecy and a warning in 1922—a prophecy which was then in process of being summarily fulfilled in part and some years later vindicated in full measure. But England refused to be excited. One man was for socialized medicine and cared not for the other issues. If you told him that was socialism he replied: "That is just playing with a word." Another was for taking over the coal mines from a boss he hated. He cared not what name you gave it. One group was for one thing; another group was for something else. They did not realize that all these things together added up to socialism, and that this would bring great alterations in the shape and habits of the society in which they lived and included many things besides soaking the rich and substituting a London bureau as boss for the one they had. Far the greater number were labor union members following the

[4] "Where Are We Going?" by David Lloyd George, Doran, 1923.

union line. Security was the existing bait and those who called these things socialism were denounced for using the word.

It comes about that a crucial moment turns up in the history of a people when its future course may hang upon the decision of one man or a few. Such a moment arrived in England in 1923. And such a moment is sure to arrive in this country involving precisely the same circumstances. In the election of that year, the Conservatives won. This seemed to indicate that Lloyd George's prophecy was without foundation. The flood had not come after all. But the Conservatives did not elect enough members to give them a majority in the House of Commons. They had 258 members. The Laborites were second with 191. The Liberals were last with 158. Asquith, the Liberal leader, could throw his votes to the Conservatives and put them in power, or to the Laborites. At this point he made a historic decision which settled the fate of the Liberal Party forever. He threw its votes to the Labor Party and made the Socialist, Ramsay MacDonald, Prime Minister. "It was better," he said, "to install a Labor Government with its claws cut as the best insurance against a fighting Labor Government." He added: "The experiment could hardly be made under safer conditions." Lord Grey, who had been Liberal Foreign Secretary, said: "I regard the advent of a Labor government under these circumstances with no apprehension at all."

Thus only 18 years after the start, literally from scratch, of the Socialist drive, their leader was England's Prime Minister. Instead of cutting the claws of the Labor government, Asquith had cut the throat of the Liberal Party. Asquith's Liberals and Stanley Baldwin's Conservative voters represented a vast majority of the people. But Asquith turned the machinery of the British Empire over to the Socialist Labor Party representing only a third of the electorate and with only 191 votes out of 615 seats in the Commons. After that the Liberals would dwindle until in the last election of 1945 they elected only 11 members. Of course, in 1923 MacDonald did not remain long in power. The Conservatives succeeded to office very quickly and retained the government until 1929.

But what had happened to England? The Socialists were pointing to what they called the bankruptcy of the Capitalist system. Certainly the British Capitalist system was sadly disarranged. There were two reasons for this. England's economy had been built upon her empire and her foreign trade. The war had shaken this to its foundations. England was like a greengrocer whose neighborhood had been partly wrecked. What failed was the world in which England traded. Her foreign policy had imposed upon her a burden she could no longer support. It had plunged her into a great war which had left her weighed down under a destructive external national debt. This was the contribution her Tories had made to her troubles.

The second cause of her difficulties represented the contribution of her Socialists. They had imposed upon her a crushing burden of social services that was impoverishing the government. In 1924-25 the government spent 792 million pounds. Of this nearly half—357 million pounds—was consumed by her debt. She spent 111 million pounds on defense and *178 million pounds on her Socialist social services*. The ordinary expenses of government were only 148 million. Social services, debt and defense consumed 646 million pounds. It should take no wizard in public finance to predict what the fate of such a government would be. It was not capitalism that was failing. It was Britain's kind of capitalism, crushed under the weight of her crumbling imperialism, her "victorious" war and her Socialist spenders.

At the next election in 1929 the Labor Party for the first time had the largest number of seats in the Commons, though short of a majority. By now the English people had had their fears of socialism definitely allayed. The terrors of Marxian revolution and of the complete confiscation of property had vanished. The Labor Party made it clear it had no intention of seizing their farms, their stores, their factories. It was only the great industries, the basic industries, that would be taken—steel, coal, railways. These belonged to the rich. As for the workers, they would get more pay, shorter hours, free medicine, pensions, benefits of all sorts. The plan took on an aspect of benevolence that allayed the fears and captivated the imagination of the working classes of England.

However, by this time—1929—the great depression had spread its black pinions over the world. The Socialist leaders did what they would have denounced the Conservatives for doing. They cut the dole and raised taxes. The Labor Party denounced them, whereupon MacDonald resigned. A new coalition cabinet was formed with MacDonald at its head, made up of Laborites, Conservatives and two Liberals. The Labor Party expelled its four top leaders. Three million Britons were out of work. Herbert Morrison, Laborite leader, said dolefully: "Social reform of capitalism has its limitations." He might have said more truthfully that reform of capitalism by Socialists not only has its limitations but is impossible. This was one of the gravest maladies of all Europe. So-called Capitalist nations were being run by Socialist governments whose leaders did not believe in capitalism, and, at intervals, by Capitalist leaders who were trying desperately to get Socialist support at the polls to remain in power. Of course after 1935 when Hitler was in full career, England and all Europe began to rearm, with the usual luminous bubble of armament prosperity and, I may add, the inevitable climax of every such episode in human history—war.

The First World War had hit Britain a smashing blow from which she never recovered, despite a brief interval of seeming convalescence. The Second World War struck her a thundering blast of epic violence. Her commonwealth remained but her empire withered away. Her foreign trade disappeared. Her economic system lay in ruins. She herself went on the dole with billions in handouts from America. To say that any Capitalist government had anything to offer other than sweat and short rations for a decade at least was to ignore realities. Only the Socialist had his radiant rainbow ready, his promises of the good life, jobs for all, security for all from the cradle to the grave. And so when Churchill called for a general election in 1945 the inevitable happened. The Labor Party saw the seemingly happy climax of its long years of scheming, promising and pious deceptions. It won 394 seats in the Commons against

216 for the Conservatives and only 11 for the pathetic remnant
of the Liberal Party which had made Labor's rise possible.

But even in this climax the people as a whole did not compre-
hend the full meaning of their decision. They were not voting
for socialism with its whole cargo of social and economic doctrines and arrangements. Margaret Cole, the wife of G. D. H.
Cole, in *Harper's* Magazine (July, 1948), admits that "basically
the two great issues of the 1945 election were Social Security—
which means that the poor shall not perish from their poverty—
and Fair Shares for All . . . The idea that neither poverty nor
lack of suitable parents should handicap a citizen . . ." They did
not envision all the harsh and inevitable implications of the grim
Socialist State. But, for all that, the Socialist-captained Labor
Party had finally achieved its aims.

1. It had captured the labor unions which paid its bills and
supplied most of its votes.

2. It had penetrated the Liberal Party and destroyed it.

3. It had built its Labor Party and replaced its old Liberal
ally.

4. It had carefully soft-pedalled the word socialism and put
its emphasis on labor objectives and social security institutions.

5. It had begun with the Welfare State and moved in from
there.

6. It had penetrated the educational and intellectual institutions of the country, including the church, all of which had become its powerful allies.

7. It had led the electorate along one step at a time until the
Capitalist part of the social machine was gravely impaired and
the Socialist part began to emerge as the dominant factor. In
1945 it crowned its long creeping revolution with a success
which amazed its own leaders. Socialism took power in Great
Britain.

The hour had arrived when the promises were no longer
acceptable. The stern day of performance was at hand. For
four years the Socialist prophets of abundance have been struggling with their contract. And quite suddenly it has begun to
dawn upon the people of England that the realities of the So-

cialist paradise do not correspond with the dream. Suddenly this new condition that was hailed as the Brave New World of the Future has acquired a new name—given to it by its own followers. It is called "Austerity." Its militant leader, Sir Stafford Cripps, is now known to his legions not as Lord Bountiful but as Mr. Austerity. He can offer his troubled people only taxes, rations and compulsions. The dream is turning into a nightmare, as we shall see in the succeeding chapter before we apply the lessons of this brief British history to our own case.

CHAPTER THREE

The Socialist Reality

To UNDERSTAND what has happened in Britain we must be clear about the use of words. We must know what socialism means in England. We continue to use the words "communism" and "socialism" as describing two generically different ideas. As a matter of fact, the words were interchangeable until the Russian revolution. One thing we can be clear about: Russia is a Socialist country and Britain is a Socialist country. There are, however, differences between Socialists. They differ about the method of achieving socialism, about the extent to which a country's industries should be nationalized and about the forms of administration.

The word communism had fallen more or less into disuse before the First World War. Lenin revived it as he prepared for his final assault on Russia. He had become disgusted with the softer approach of the old Social-Democrats (a favorite name for Socialist parties in Europe). He insisted that for Russia there could be no democratic approach. He was for a revolution and insisted on a complete break with the less robust Socialist techniques. "To emphasize his complete break with the past," says Shub in his recent absorbing life of the Russian leader, "Lenin urged dropping the name Social Democratic Party in favor of the Communist Party." [1]

We have now got into the habit of using the word communism to describe the Russian organization. But that organization is a Socialist one. The Russians call themselves Socialists. The great scripture of world socialism is called the "Communist Manifesto." But Marx and Engels, who wrote it, called

[1] "Lenin, A Biography" by David Shub, Doubleday, 1948.

themselves Socialists. The Russians style their country the Union of Soviet *Socialist* Republics. Actually these two words describe the Marxian collectivist philosophy which asserts the right of the State to assume complete control over the economic fabric of society. Socialists and Communists may differ as to the extent and character of the control but we must not let this obscure the fact that they are all Socialists.

Socialist propagandists from Britain never fail to impress on Americans that they have socialized only about 25 per cent of the economic system and that 75 per cent remains under capitalism. This is a clever distortion of the facts. Britain has "nationalized" about 25 per cent of her economic processes. But she has "socialized" nearly the entire economic system. In Russia the Socialists took over everything for State operation. In Britain the State has socialized eight great basic industries or services by taking them over under State operation. The rest of the system they have socialized under the method of economic planning. The State asserts the authority to make the plans for all forms of business—farms, factories, mines, shops. It decides on production quotas for an industry as a whole and in many cases for the individual units in the industry. It fixes the quotas and priorities on which raw materials are distributed, fixes prices at which they are bought and sold, fixes labor quotas and wages, determines who shall get credit at the banks and who shall not, and generally makes the blueprints upon which all business operations are carried on and polices those operations to ensure faithful obedience to its plans.

In short, the government takes over the general planning and direction of all industry. And in the exercise of this authority it decides which industries ought to be nationalized and operated directly by the State and which should be left in the hands of private owners to carry on under State planning and supervision. As part of this latter function the State, by taxation, takes the greater part of whatever profits are possible in such a system. This is the system now in use in Great Britain. Here is how it works.

The government has nationalized eight functions:

1. The Bank of England.
2. Cables and wireless—the overseas communications system.
3. Civil aviation.
4. Transport, which includes the railways, road transport (buses and cargo transport) and inland waterways.
5. Coal mines.
6. Electricity.
7. Gas industry.
8. Medical services.

The House of Commons has voted to nationalize the iron and steel industry but this has not yet been passed by the House of Lords and will not be until next year, if at all, depending perhaps on the result of the next elections.

The remainder of the economic structure, including factories, farms, housing, stores, shipping is being operated by private owners under the government controls, which may be compared to those controls that were in force during the war both here and in England with their priorities, quotas, subsidies, price-fixing, rationing, inspections and penalties—all enforced by an army of bureaucrats—save that they are more onerous in England under socialism now than they were there during the war.

However, the Socialists have no intention of permitting all this to remain in private hands indefinitely. Michael Young, Research Director of the British Labor Party, admits that the constitution of the Labor Party commits it to public ownership of the means of production, distribution and exchange—which means practically everything. And he also admits that a section of the party wishes to rush on to the completion of this program. Herbert Morrison and his faction favor consolidating the present plans before moving on. But there is no escaping the fact that they intend to move on. Mr. Young says that those things "scheduled for public ownership are water supply, mineral deposits, meat wholesaling and processing, cold storage, the sugar industry, the cement industry and, most controversial of all, industrial life insurance." He adds "this is not all" and that shipbuilding and sections of the chemical industries will also be nationalized. He declares that factories will be built by the State and leased to private concerns in what is left of the private sector. Machinery will be *rented* by the government to manufacturers. Public finance corporations will lend money for equipment. And if the government decides the private operators are not producing efficiently then the government will set up competing plants. There is still another device, which is called "socialization of demand." It is also called "bulk purchasing." This means the government will buy up the total output of factories and dispose of it to consumers, thus eliminating the merchant.[2]

What has all this done for and to Britain? If the British Socialist experiment were successful, one would suppose that it would have produced more goods at lower prices and each worker would be getting a larger share of the world's goods than under the old Capitalist regime. The people would be freer and happier and the security--the real security—of the nation would be advanced in every way.

These longed-for consequences have not appeared. By every test—political and economic, physical and moral—British socialism has been a tragic failure. It is already falling apart. Everything goes wrong. The people cry out against impossible prices, scarcities in almost everything, scandalously oppressive taxation, bureaucratic sluggards and oppressors. Britain's foreign trade—the foundation of her economic existence--is being washed away. Even with the aid of billions from Capitalist America she cannot settle her foreign debts save by the slow extinction of her gold reserves. And as for the moral order, her people have seen those great freedoms for which Englishmen have fought through the centuries slowly withering away— freedom from seizures and searches without warrants, freedom to work where and at what they choose, freedom to engage in business and to own property, freedom to work their privately owned farms as they choose. Let us look at the black record.

The industries and functions which the Socialist government

[2] "British Labor's New Five Year Plan" by Michael Young, *New Republic*, April 25, 1949.

has taken over it has operated at a loss. And it has failed either
to improve the services or increase the output in these nationalized enterprises. In the coal mines it was, at the end of
1948, producing 158,000 tons a week or 7,000,000 tons a year
less than the mines under private ownership produced before
the war, notwithstanding the expenditure by the Socialist government of over 170 million dollars on mechanization to increase per-man output. It has been discovered and admitted that
the miners, notwithstanding the oily fiction that they are now
the "owners" of the mines, will not produce any more for themselves than they produced before the war for private owners.

In spite of increased mechanization, particularly in cutting
machinery, per-man output is less than it was in 1938 and, odd-
est of all, absenteeism has increased. Around 84,000 miners a
day fail to show up. The cost of producing coal has risen from
16 shillings a ton in 1938 to 46 shillings in 1948. The National
Coal Board lost around $95,000,000 in 1947. By raising the price
of coal it managed barely to cover costs in 1948 but is still in the
red for about $90,000,000 since it began operations. The Coal
Board has warned of the grave threat involved in these facts.
"Coal used in the manufacture of British goods," it says, "may
make them too dear to compete with goods from other countries." This is precisely what is happening.

The government owns the overseas air transport industry
and this it has operated, in the Atlantic area, at a loss of $244
on every passenger carried, while paying its employees little
more than half that earned by the employees of its American
competitor. The railroads have been run at a substantial deficit.
The losses suffered on each new industry taken over were em-
barrassing at first. But now some of the government apologists are
saying that losses are of no consequence. Of course every loss
sustained by the government on one of its enterprises must be
paid by the government, which can get the money for that purpose only from taxes—taxes on the meat and bread and clothing
and necessities of the ordinary people of England. There are not
now enough rich left to soak with any results. There are only 45
persons in England whose incomes after taxes exceed $24,000 a

tomers. They must be prices at which she can compete against her trade rivals in foreign markets. She certainly will never be able to sell at low prices abroad goods which she produces at a loss at home. And she never will be able to sell other goods abroad when the prices of those goods must include the enormous taxes of the Socialist government.

She will never be able to produce cheaply in industries operated by the government. And private industries will never be able to produce cheaply when they must include in their costs the enormous taxes which the government takes out of them as its share. This regime of the Socialists may be able to drag along only so long as it can collect free billions in aid from private-enterprise America. When that ceases—as it must—England's Socialist government will stand face to face with the grim realities. But it is entirely possible that even with this aid the day of reckoning may come—possibly before this book can leave the presses.

The end of American help may come sooner than expected. England is getting this aid not from an American capitalism in a state of robust health, but from an American capitalism heavily drugged by artificial stimulants, loaded with debt, watered down with Socialist ingredients and facing a slump because of these factors. If there is one prayer the devout British Socialist should send up nightly to the Giver of All Good Things, it is that God will save America from drifting into socialism.

Of course the bait held out by the Socialists to the workers was the vision of a softer and more abundant life. Michael Straight, the Socialist editor of the *New Republic*, writes that "the workers dreamed that on the day they took power, the slums would somehow turn into bright communities, the hidden horde of the Capitalist treasure would be unearthed and divided among all. The age of plenty had come." This radiant dream was of course dissolved in the reality of the Socialist nightmare. It does not, however, prevent the Socialist propagandists from peddling here these spurious pictures of the happy Socialist isle.

John Vandercook, Socialist commentator, writes that "the standard of living of the great majority has risen to the highest level since the beginning of the industrial revolution." For all practical purposes, he reports, real poverty has been abolished and the most astonishing phenomenon in Britain is the "relative enrichment of the poor." This is merely repeating what Prime Minister Attlee had said in a moment of carelessness. He declared in a speech that the standard of living of "the great majority of the people had risen to its highest peak." But he said this to Englishmen who knew better and who promptly raised such a storm of protest that this foolish boast had to be quickly watered down. And two months later John Strachey, Minister of Food, revised it by saying that, "The *bottom third* of the population is better fed now than before the war." Professor Jewkes' rejoinder to this, in his account of England's Ordeal by Planning, was that this meant merely that "The bottom third was actually below the poverty line" and that the other two-thirds was at or near the poverty line. Poverty had not been abolished. It had been distributed. A small minority had been brought up a little. The great majority had been grievously brought down.

Then Strachey invented a new boast, that the British people "are getting enough money to buy all the food they ought to have." But, alas, the Minister is the judge of "what they ought to have." And here is the permitted ration: one egg and a half a week, three ounces of butter, six ounces of margarine, one ounce of lard, one ounce of cheese, one ounce of bacon, eight ounces of sugar, six ounces of meat, two ounces of corn beef. This is Socialist abundance four years after the war had ended. The British indeed do have more money, a result which has been accomplished by the ancient trick of inflating the currency. They have expanded the money supply and diminished the food supply.

One of their boasts is true. They do have "full employment." So did Hitler, Mussolini and so has Stalin. Everyone is employed in England. But millions of employed are worse off than those on relief in America and some malignant economic law seems to be forcing the whole body of the population lower and lower in the standard of living. All work, but production lags and "fair shares for all"—the happy Socialist election slogan in 1945

—has turned out to be merely an ever dwindling share in less and less. The *New Statesman*, which is by no means a captious critic of Planning, says: "You may have social security, but you cannot go into a store and buy two quarts of milk:" To which an English commentator replies: "You not only cannot buy two quarts of milk. You cannot buy one. You can only get two quarts of milk on your doorstep a week. If you try to get more you are apt to land in jail."

We are informed that wages have risen splendidly and Vandercook reports that the number getting from $12 to $40 a week has increased from something over six million to a little over 13 million. This is quite true, I daresay, but this rise took place, as he admits, before the Socialists took power and, of course, as a result of the war inflation. Wages have increased but so have prices. Vandercook insists prices have not risen as high as wages but he also admits that this is because the government makes a contribution of $2.50 a week to every family's grocery bill through the food subsidies which, of course, are paid from taxes out of every family's income.

The great boast is the social services—from the cradle to the grave—$16 at birth and $80 for a Christian burial. Indeed they begin before birth with pre-natal care and cover medical care, hospitalization, old-age retirement payments, unemployment insurance, allowances for widows and for families in need. The allowances, however, are meager, and merely a "cushion against complete disaster" and a "pretty thin one" says Vandercook. But thin as they are, these social services, along with the losses on the nationalized industries, and the cost of the bulging bureaucracy are wrecking the enervated economic structure of England. All these immense payments must be met by taxes and these taxes must be extracted from the national income, which means they show up in the price of the things England has to sell abroad with disastrous consequences to the export business which is the very blood supply of her economy.

The shallowest illusion of the workers was that socialism would end "wage slavery." The old Socialist visionaries like Annie Besant said, and believed, that "laziness would disappear" when men worked for the Socialist State. But in fact the worker has now merely exchanged the old boss for a new bureaucrat. The old boss might have been a tough fellow, but he might also have been a fairly decent human being and most of them were. The boss now is a cold, impersonal being, full of theoretical humanity, far away in London and no decision can be made by any small foreman on the job without an immense amount of paper work that begins at the local office and moves snail-like through various local boards, sub-councils, regional boards and other bureaucratic nests up to London and finally back through the same succession of petty bureaus. Decisions are made by inflexible rule, with the human element extracted as, for instance, the laying off of a coal miner just a month before his pension would accrue and the bald refusal to reinstate him for the extra month to hold on to the benefit he had put in 20 years accumulating. At the annual conference of colliery managers, the chairman complained to the National Coal Board of a lack of humanity in dealing with the staffs. Short, staccato, impersonal orders in stereotyped letters have taken the place of the friendly, personal correspondence between managers and the boss. There is, he complained, "a general atmosphere of distrust and caution in speech between one person and another which never existed before."

Added to all this is the sinister consequence of the controls. The condition of the people in this respect is worse than during the war. Regulations and amended regulations pour from the presses daily so that neither shopkeeper nor housewife can keep up with them. If you kick you are called anti-social. If you disobey you may land in jail. There were 30,000 prosecutions for infractions of the regulations in a single year. This may be endured in war-time. In peace-time it is intolerable.

Mr. Williams admits the workers are not producing as much for the State they supposedly love as they did for the boss they were supposed to hate. He admits "there is not much evidence that nationalization has altered the attitude of the workers as radically as was hoped or has created any definite feeling of partnership in a national enterprise." And as for the boss who rode him in the old days, now it means "to the ordinary worker not, as he had expected, an easier time, but an appeal to work harder than ever before—without much obvious recompense either in increased control over his own destiny during his working life or in the feeling that he is no longer simply an employee but 'one of the owners.'" [4]

And what about his chances of getting ahead? Mr. Williams also admits there is nothing yet to make the workers in the factory feel that "socialism has given them any bigger share than they had in running things."

But there is yet something infinitely more important. All this is in the domain of dollars and wages and economic regulations. There are the things of the spirit which are the core of our culture. And one of these has to do with that thing for which Britons for over a thousand years have fought battles and spilled rivers of blood. It is human freedom. One part of this freedom is the liberty an Englishman enjoyed of doing with his life what he wished—seeking his happiness and his welfare where he thought he might find it best. It was his freedom not merely to own a farm or to start a business but to work wherever any man might be willing to give him a job. Freedom of occupation, we might call this one. This is one of the great basic rights which the Soviet tyranny has abolished under Russian socialism.

Being Englishmen, the Socialist leaders declared fervently they would never interfere with the right of British working men to choose their occupations. The brief history of how these libertarians slowly bowed before the grim necessities of the system they sought to manage has been reviewed by Professor John Jewkes of the University of Manchester. [5]

Sir Stafford Cripps in February, 1946, faced this situation boldly. He admitted that every country which has attempted a planned economy had been compelled to use compulsion of labor. "Our objective," he declared, "is to carry through a

[4] *Ibid.*
[5] "Ordeal by Planning" by John Jewkes, Macmillan, 1948. I suggest to the reader who wishes a clear and authoritative examination of the British Socialist experiment that he could not do better than to study carefully this excellent book.

planned economy *without compulsion of labor*." (Italics added.) His critics insisted this was impossible. However, by the Fall of 1947, the British Planners discovered their plans were going awry. Cripps must have felt a sense of desperation.

Adequate supplies of labor and full effort by workmen were not forthcoming in the industries the government wished to stimulate. Cripps made an appeal to the workers. He begged them to consider if what they were producing were the things the country most needed. He told them they had no right to complain about shortages of coal and underclothing and housing when they refused to work in sufficient numbers in these industries. The appeal fell on deaf ears—not wicked ears, but the ears of ordinary working people who, by the very limitations of nature, cannot escape making the decisions affecting their habits and conduct in time of peace upon highly practical premises based on their personal and family interests. Great numbers of miners refused to work more than four days a week. Even high pay failed to tempt workers away from their accustomed crafts or their home towns.

And so in the end Sir Stafford and his colleagues had to yield to the inevitable and enact a law which says that *no man between the ages of 18 and 50, or woman between the ages of 18 and 40, could change occupations at will. The Minister of Labor had the power to direct such workers to the employment he considered best for the national interest*. This is the notorious "Control of Engagements" Act. Professor Jewkes observes that the "government had the choice between freedom of occupation and planning, and they chose planning." And he notes that the Prime Minister in February, 1947, had said that 17 ministries had power to enter private homes for inspections without a search warrant and that over 10,000 officials had the power to make such entries!

No end of devious apology has been offered for this dark stain on Britain's shield. Mr. Walter Scott-Elliot, M.P., wrote the London *Times* on June 16, 1949, minimizing the character of this compulsive order. Oddly, he ruled out "compulsion" as fit only for the totalitarian state, and he insisted the Control of

Engagements Order was not "compulsion." He points out that the Order provides that a worker can obtain work in only one way—by applying to the local office of the Ministry of Labor. This puts him, as to a job, wholly at the mercy of the Minister. The choice would be, in the first instance, between the job offered by the Ministry and starvation. But refusal may be treated as a public offense. The Minister may seek to guide the applicant to work "into an industry where he can best serve the national interest." But he admits that in the end, "The Minister of Labor *has power to issue directions*." And he adds that "this power *is seldom* exercised"—which means, of course, it is exercised upon occasion. It has been exercised and men have been put in jail for resisting it. Exercising it often is obviously not necessary.

This rudimentary muscle of ruthlessness does not stop at the factory. It has made its way to the farm. Over the head of the farmer hangs a threat perhaps more serious than that applied to the worker. The farmers are paid heavy subsidies to produce more food. But there is a regular inspection of every farm and a record kept of its produce. If the farmer falls short of the kind of job expected of him in following the instructions from London he gets a warning and if he does not mend his ways the government will walk in, put a price upon his property, pay him for it and put him off the farm, which then passes into the hands of a government manager.

The article in the New York *Times* of May 1, 1949, which records this dismal fact adds by way of comment: "This does not happen very often because the farmers work together to discipline each other, *but it has happened often enough to keep 99 per cent of English farmers in line*." In return for this the farmer gets higher prices for his product through government subsidies. In addition to this stroke of the Russian knout, he pays high prices for what he buys, recently was confronted by an increase of $40 a ton on the feed he uses and has the wages of his workers fixed by the government so that many farmers say they would be better off without help. And then, of course, there are the taxes.

In July, 1949, Robert Wallace Bell, Justice of the Peace of Colts Crofts, Acton, Suffolk, refused to pay his assessment on the national insurance scheme. He is a retired officer of the Indian police. He declared that many persons—clergymen and pensioners who are not yet 65—suffer the utmost hardship from this act because they literally cannot find the money to pay the levies. He refused to pay as a protest. One might suppose the government could sue him or perhaps revoke or impair his pension rights. But the Justice was arrested and fined 10 pounds at Boxford and an additional 4 pounds, 13 shillings in contributions and three guineas in costs. Had he been unable to pay he would have been sent to jail—for defaulting on an insurance payment. This is a sample.

These British Socialist Planners who have done these things are not wicked men. They are, however, men who are convinced they know how to run a whole nation of human beings who have been taught by an age-old tradition that their most priceless heritage is human freedom. The leaders have discovered, in installments, that this cannot be done without applying compulsions to labor and farmers as well as to industrial proprietors—something they said devoutly they would never do. They have learned, if the system they have planned is to endure much longer, that they must either become ruthless themselves or give way in favor of successors who will not shrink from ruthlessness.

Need we be surprised at this? Twenty years ago Hilaire Belloc, peering into the future of the promised British socialism in practice, said: "Two things are likely. (1) Compulsory labor will come and (2) it will be called some name not remotely connected with the idea of slavery or compulsion of labor." He suggested courts would be set up to try unwilling workers but these would doubtless be called "loyalty" courts. One of the curses of this whole system is that nothing is called by an honest name. Words are used to deceive and not to enlighten. Hateful practices, abhorred for ages by a free people, are now identified by luminous words, while acts and practices thought to be proper and even praiseworthy are ticketed by the most odious names. The man who works in a privately owned factory is a wage slave. Socialism itself is never called socialism. It is National Planning. Thrift is a vice until the government asks you to save and lend it money, when it becomes a virtue. And the most diabolical crime against society is profit. Winston Churchill recently observed that the real crime against society was not profit but loss. Private industry runs at a profit and uses the profit to expand producing capacity. Government industry runs at a loss and taxes the substance of the people to pay for its inefficiencies. Which is the greater crime against society?

Yet the old Socialists who set all this in motion did not foresee what the end would be. They supposed that the one thing essential to complete the Briton's freedom was to get the land and machines out of the hands of the Capitalist exploiter and into the hands of the people. Then the last bastion of liberty would be won. But the socialism they talked was a dream. It was not something that had been tried and proved. It had no history of performance. It was just a gleaming promise. I remember when the old Czarist regime collapsed in Russia and the Kerensky government took power there. I recall the joy that filled the hearts of the American Socialists. I remember sitting in the old Rialto Theatre in New York watching the moving pictures of the sailors and soldiers and people marching in the streets with their banners hailing the dawn of freedom. I saw men all around me weeping at this incredible liberation and I could not restrain the tears myself. How little they suspected the harsh reality that would rise out of that glorious redemption and spread its dark influence all over eastern Europe.

The men who began this experiment in England also were moved by the dream of a wider and fuller freedom. But the fact remains that those who are in power are after all only men and what they have hold of is not a dream but a grim reality and that as the terrible necessities of their experiment have challenged them they have not hesitated to scrap first one and then another of the spiritual elements in their dream. It will always be so. Liberty will always be the first victim in every plan to concentrate vast powers in a central State run by men and not by angels. That is why there are more slaves in the world today than there were before the war to end slavery.

As we attempt a judgment on England and on the plans afoot in our own country we will do well to be clear as to what we mean by freedom. Our great Declaration has defined the institution of human freedom as the "right to life, liberty and the pursuit of happiness." What does this involve? It involves the right to choose our rulers and the corollary right to keep out of the hands of those rulers the means of interfering with our free choice. It includes the right to speak our minds, to have access to the means of information, to be free from arrest and search without the authorized warrant of law, to choose where we shall live, to own property, to choose our form of occupation and to spend our incomes as we think best.

In exercising these freedoms we are, of course, limited by the freedoms and the natural rights of others. But they include the right to make the wrong decisions in the exercise of each of them. The pursuit of happiness consists in using our lives as we think best so long as we do not infringe the same right in others, to work a great deal or only a little, while seeking our happiness in whatever profitable or unprofitable avocation seems best for us. It includes the right to use our incomes wisely or foolishly; to spend them or invest them. What is the wise way to use them? To open a little store or take over a farm or go fishing or buy books to read, to travel or just save? No State can look into the depths of a man's mind and heart and assay those intangible spiritual elements in him which are the springs of his happiness. And we must be reminded that in all the debate and oratory about freedom this right to the "pursuit of happiness" is being very generally omitted from the problem.

It is this great attribute of freedom with which the British Socialists have been tinkering. It was inevitable. Years ago many of the early Socialists rebelled on this very point and insisted that the Socialist State, uniting the functions of political ruler, landlord and employer of the population, would bring into existence the most complete and appalling tyranny conceivable. This is what has happened in Russia. These skeptics left the

Socialist organization and invented a form of society which would put the instruments of production in the hands of syndicates of workers and practically abolish the State. These were the Syndicalists, who were our I.W.W.'s in the America of 1900.

Now the British Socialist, faced with the problem of compelling the Englishman to comply with his plans, has turned his hand to compulsions. The government has plenty of machinery for this, since it now possesses electric power, transportation, credit and fuel—without which no man can operate a business. The government can grant or withhold these. But it has gone much further. It asserts the right to tell a man where he shall work or not work and even to force him to change his habitation from one part of England to another. It still permits him to own or to buy land, though where he will get the money to buy in the future I do not know. And, of course, part of the Socialist program is ultimately to take all the land and transform every Briton into a State tenant. His right to spend his income as he chooses is almost permanently abolished, since the government takes so much of it in taxes that the vast mass of the people have no more left than will cover the bare necessities of life.

It is of striking interest that Francis Williams, an ardent apologist of the British Labor Party, concedes that national planning, involving so much government power, "brings with it such an extension of controls which may, if great care is not exercised, eat away small liberties, even though they leave the big ones untouched." He freely admits it is a danger in planned societies against "which they need constantly to be on their guard" and he confesses his fear "that the Labor government has not always been as watchful as they might have been." He ends his book on this note: That what they are seeking is a world without hedges. A classless and towerless world. A world where men may write freely and live freely and find a common belief that they can share. A world also in which they can have a lot of fun.[6]

[6] "Socialist Britain" by Francis Williams.

Here is an odd dream indeed. A planned world! A world
without hedges planned and run by professional hedge-build-
ers, by men whose passion is to build towers for themselves and
fences for the whole population, and road blocks and traffic
lights on every highway and side street of human activity.
Britain is only at the beginning of this book. As the difficulties
grow greater, as the grumblings of the multitude rise in volume, the benevolent men like Attlee and Morrison and their
sort will move out of the picture and the sterner planners will
move in. Already Mr. Aneurin Bevan, the strident and demanding Minister of Health, has startled England with a touch of
ruthlessness. Suddenly the Labor Party has been confronted
with the possibility of a Conservative victory in 1950. Mr.
Bevan, speaking at a Labor meeting at Blackpool (June 6, 1949),
said:

> "If there was a Tory majority at the next election Great
> Britain would have said to the world, 'The road to progress by
> means of democratic government is closed. The British have
> said it. The most assured, self-reliant and sophisticated people
> in the world have tried the instrument of representative gov-
> ernment and have failed. There is nothing therefore left. All
> the roads are closed except the roads to tyranny and oppres-
> sion. All the roads are closed except the roads to civil war. All
> the roads are closed except to the blood bath that is the his-
> tory of mankind.' "

There it is—stark and challenging. If the voice of the majority speaks at the next election—that democratic majority
which the Socialists extoll—then this minister of the Crown,
who is often mentioned as the next Prime Minister, declares the
only appeal will be to the "blood bath of history." Let us be
under no misapprehensions. The present ministry has among its
members men who are prepared to move into the seats of power
and use those weapons of compulsion from which Kerensky
shrank but which Lenin took up, from which Attlee and Morrison and Cripps may shrink, but from which Aneurin Bevan
will not turn.

It would be possible to fill a small book with accounts, both amusing and terrifying, of the blunders of men who assume that they know how to plan the operations of a whole people. In 1947, Mr. Shinwell, then Minister of Fuel and Power, told the House of Commons that he had ordered all electricity for trade shut off in London and the Midlands and the extensive industrial areas around these two sections. The immediate consequence of this was to shut down 75 per cent of British industry. The reason given was the shortage of coal for producing electricity. It would last, said the Minister, only two or three days. But it actually lasted three weeks. It threw 2,000,000 people out of work and lost over $800,000,000 in export trade so desperately needed. Why was no provision made against the coal shortage? So many people predicted it that Shinwell said in the Commons: "Everybody knows we are going to have a coal shortage except the Minister." He denied it, but it came and he shut down the entire power-using industry in a great industrial area.[7]

In 1946 this same Mr. Shinwell, foreseeing another coal shortage, suggested to the Minister of Transport, Mr. Alfred Barnes, that he convert 1200 locomotives to oil, thus effecting a great saving in coal. It will be observed that England has no oil and great stores of coal. Mr. Barnes went ahead and by September, 1947, he had converted 93 locomotives to oil. He had spent about $6,000,000. Oil, of course, is far more expensive than coal in England and this policy would cost, if 1200 locomotives were converted, about $16,000,000 a year more to run them. However, when the 93 locomotives were completed, Mr. Barnes made some inquiry about getting oil and discovered there was none to be had for this purpose. The British Transport Commission reversed the plan. Mr. Barnes and Mr. Shinwell now had on their hands 93 locomotives for which there was no oil and so the 93 locomotives were reconverted from oil back to coal.

In January, 1947, the great plan to house the houseless Britisher was announced by the ministry. There would be 250,000

7 "Ordeal by Planning" by John Jewkes.

houses built in the year. The government went on with the plans. Brick, cement, plumbing, nails, plaster and all sorts of things for the job were ordered and the factories went to work on them. But when all this was well along it was discovered that lumber could not be supplied for more than 60,000 houses, so the great plan had to fall short by 190,000 houses. In the meantime, all the other materials were being furiously produced. It was also discovered that there was not nearly enough labor for the purpose. Bricks in great piles were lying around in brickyards closed for lack of buyers. Other materials were piling up. And the program flopped pathetically.

These are just a few samples which can be quickly explained. We can match every one of these blunders among our American planners. When they occur the critics point to the stupidity of the planners. But I think the fault lies rather in the fact that the mind of man, which is after all a very limited instrument, is utterly inadequate for comprehending the vast amount of data and all the innumerable conditions which would have to be grasped in order to make plans for a whole nation. It simply cannot be done. It is conceivable that it may be done in some half-bungling way in a society where an absolute dictator runs the show and has the means not only of enforcing complete compliance but of shutting off all criticism. It can never be done in a society of free men where criticism cannot be silenced and where compliance cannot be enforced.

There is another frightful blunder which the Socialists have committed. In taking over the railroads, the coal industry and others, they have bought the properties outright from the corporations and stockholders who owned them. They have paid for them with British bonds paying three per cent interest. With each new industry taken over, the government has added another mass of obligations to its already crushing national debt. Now the folly of this lies in the fact that, under the old order, the stockholders had no claim for profit if none were made by the industry. But all these stocks—pure risk investments—have been converted into government bonds—which are a fixed charge upon the government, whether the industry makes a profit or not. And as all these industries have been operating at a greater or lesser loss, the government has had to find in taxes the means of paying this debt. Indeed it has been charged in the United States Senate that the British government had got permission from the United States Commission to use $82,000,000 of the American funds granted Britain to pay interest on its debt which it was unable to meet because of the additions to it created by these nationalization schemes.

Thus the great Socialist experiment which was going to liquidate the greedy Capitalist profit-maker has now set him up as a tax-supported institution with the risk taken out of his investment, literally endowing him in perpetuity with his three per cent no matter what happens. However, it may not turn out that way. The hard days are coming in England. The coal miners want more money and they are now crying out in angry terms for suspending or abolishing the compensation of the former owners.

There is no room here to describe what might be a gigantic comedy if it were not so grave a tragedy—the experiment in socialized medicine in England. That great numbers of people in Britain were not receiving adequate medical attention cannot be denied. What Britain needed was more medical care. That is, the task was to preserve what she had and then take measures to expand the personnel and equipment to cover more people. What she has done is not to increase the instrumentalities for medical care but to spread what she had out so thin that what she has now is medical care that is inadequate for almost everybody. It amounts actually to a rationing of doctors with the result that it is literally impossible for the doctors to give anybody adequate care.

Meantime, England is being taxed to death. Here is the tax return of a clerk with an income of $2800 a year. He gets a deduction of $560, an additional deduction of $720 for his wife and $480 for his two children. Total deductions: $1760. This leaves $1040 of his income subject to taxation. And here is the score:

On the first $200 he pays 15 per cent	$ 30.
On the next $800 he pays 30 per cent	240.
On the next $40 he pays 45 per cent	18.
Total tax	$ 288.

The same man with the same family and salary in the United States would pay $26. If the English clerk goes to the pub for a glass of beer to forget his troubles he pays a tax of 16 cents on the pint. If the family goes to a movie and pays 80 cents each for a seat, half of it is for the government. He need not trouble himself about furs and jewelry, but anyone who has enough to spend for them pays a tax of 100 per cent. These taxes go to pay for school meals, industrial injuries, poor relief, family allowances, plus over a billion dollars for the socialized medicine which Sir Stafford Cripps says is "free," another $1,800,000,000 for social insurance, $2,000,000,000 for food subsidies, and more billions for defense, old-age pensions, housing subsidies and debt services.

Whether or not these are good or bad, the fact remains that they cost money. And this bitter truth has now come home to the people with sudden and startling realism. The working man has been coddled with the shallow delusion that somehow all the blessed services he wanted could be paid for by soaking the rich. But the Socialist leaders found themselves at a point when it became necessary to take their beloved workers on their knees and communicate to them the harsh facts of life.

Up to April 6, 1949, outwardly at least all seemed to be going as merrily as a wedding bell in Britain. The Socialists were getting all the favorable publicity in America. Where a Socialist seat in Parliament was contested, they had won every by-election since 1945. We were being fed a pleasant stream of propaganda about the increased production and the bright outlook ahead. Then suddenly on April 6, as if some stage manager had blown a whistle and the scenes had shifted and the play had opened upon a wholly new act, the great story of Socialist Britain turned swiftly from a happy romance to a troubled and turbulent drama. That day Sir Stafford Cripps, Chancellor of the Exchequer and the intellectual leader of the Labor Party, rose in his place in the Commons and delivered his annual budget speech. The ablest of the Socialist leaders, he has in him a mixture of warm human sympathy and cold realism. It was Sir Stafford who told the workers he would never apply labor compulsions. It was Sir Stafford who did that very thing when it became necessary. As Sir Stafford began his now famous budget speech to a crowded Commons the cheers rang out from the Labor benches as he told them of Labor's achievements in the past year. Then he came to his proposals for the ensuing year. At this point a strange phenomenon occurred. His great Labor majority sat amazed and speechless, while the opposition benches did the cheering. What was it that produced this grim and resentful silence among the Socialist members?

It was the Chancellor's simple statement that now "defense and social services *must be paid for out of national income.*" He said that England has now taxed many of the rich to extinction and can get no more eggs out of that goose, that it is the worker who must bear the heavy burden of taxes now. He disclosed that England can borrow no more, that no more can be collected out of the existing national income, and that the only way government funds can be increased is by increasing the national income. The only way this can be done, he said, is by producing more and this means that the workers must work more to produce more. The great war on the rich, seemingly, has been won. They can be soaked no further. That, Sir Stafford indicated, was over.

He announced frankly that if more social services were desired they must be paid for out of taxes. "When I hear people speak of reducing taxes," he said with cold emphasis, "and at the same time see the cost of social services rising rapidly, very often in response to the demand of the same people, I wonder if they appreciate to the full the old adage: We cannot eat our cake and have it." He might have said also that the losses at which Socialist business enterprises are operated must come out of taxes too. But it would not do to put emphasis on these losses.

Sir Stafford told his colleagues that the government had been keeping food prices down by subsidizing farmers. In fact food prices were not kept down at all. The consumer was paying less but the government was paying the rest out of taxes. And this could go no further. It was costing nearly a billion and a half dollars a year and would cost two billion the coming year. The workers were nevertheless demanding lower prices for consumer goods generally, but prices could not be lowered. He said that the prices now paid for goods were insufficient to cover the cost and prices could be lowered only by having government pay a larger share, which meant more taxes. Then he announced the awful truth to the farm members, that there could be no additional subsidies, and to the industrial members that prices would have to be increased and that no further social security would be forthcoming until the workers produced more to pay for it.

There is, perhaps, no more amazing incident in parliamentary history than this one, when the majority in the House of Commons was petrified with horror at the statement of the simple fact that a nation must pay for what it gets. Nevertheless this speech—a thoroughly brilliant display of Cripps' courage—which the Conservatives cheered because he was now saying what they had been saying for years—brought only angry moans from his supporters. It was, indeed, as one Liberal member characterized it, a "budget of taxation and tears." J. H. Hudson, a Labor member, said, "It was the most appalling budget he had ever heard." Another said, "There was a lack of realism in the speech about the suffering of the people"—which implies, and justly, that the people of Socialist England are indeed suffering. Colonel Wigg, another Labor member, said the leaders would now have the greatest difficulty holding back wage increases. Mr. Blyton said the Trades Union Council was pressing for a cut in living costs and were now presented with an increase in meat prices in the face of a meat shortage "while the government was giving increased aid for health services to people who were not getting enough to eat." Butter, for one thing, was ordered increased eight cents a pound on top of a government subsidy of 26 cents a pound paid out of taxes.

Cripps said the government had begun the subsidies in order to give the people lower prices, but that they were playing with a demon. The subsidy had grown beyond anything they had contemplated. It had risen to $1,800,000,000. It might swell to half a billion more. This could not go on. And then to those elements in his party who call for more and more socialism he said:

> "We must moderate the speed of our advance in the extended application of the existing social services to our progressive ability to pay for them by an increase in our national income. Otherwise we should not be able to avoid entrenching, to an intolerable extent, on the liberty of spending by the private individual for his own purchases."

This speech produced something in the nature of a party crisis. It was a warning to the union leaders who were clamoring for higher wages. It was a demand upon the workers to work harder and produce more. It was almost an ultimatum on the question of prices and taxes. Taxes could not be raised—but they could not be lowered. It was a solemn declaration that whatever dividends the people were to get out of socialism *they must get by producing these dividends themselves*. The idea that they could get them by dividing up the wealth and the profits of the boss was no longer tenable. There might be large profits in some places but they were a drop in the bucket. The only wealth to be divided up was the wealth the workers might create themselves. It was above all a serious admonition to the over-eager warriors on the Socialist left-wing adjoining the Communists that the process of nationalization and extended social services must be slowed up, if not stopped altogether, for the time being. It set off tremendous repercussions behind the scenes in the Socialist camp.

While this row was approaching the proportions of a brawl in some quarters, the Party was brought up with a jerk by a second disaster. The nationwide elections for borough counsellors were held and to the amazement of all, including the Conservatives, the people swept over 800 Socialist members out of the local boroughs and replaced most of them with Conservatives. Borough councils that were controlled by the Socialists for years in some cases, were brought under Conservative majorities. This did not, of course, make any change in the composition of the national Parliament, but it revealed a hitherto unsuspected revolt of the voters against the government and cast an ominous shadow over the hopes of the Socialists for winning the parliamentary elections in 1950. While the politicians had been debating and the Labor leaders demanding, the great mass of the people who have been made the guinea pigs of this Socialist experiment had grown weary of the high prices and the short rations and high taxes and of the network of rules and regulations and directives in which they were snarled. Now the Socialist experimenters were suddenly confronted by a revolt of the guinea pigs. It galvanized the baffled and wobbly Conservatives into sudden optimism and activity. It changed swiftly the whole color of the political skies over England.

Hardly had this second blow fallen, when a third struck the fretful Laborites. They were preparing in May for their conference in Blackpool to settle upon the platform of principles and projects on which they would go to the country in 1950. Still disconcerted by the flinty counsel of Cripps and the harsh verdict of the voters, they now found Socialist England moving rapidly into a full scale depression. Economic law was treading upon their heels.

The Socialist promoters had made the mistake of ladling out their rosy predictions and boasts too freely. Sir Stafford Cripps' treasury secretary admitted that their followers had been led to believe "that the struggle was over." They were therefore quite bowled over as the bad news began to pour in on them almost daily. The United Press correspondent reported at the end of May that gold reserves were dwindling, export trade dropping dangerously, the stock market in a serious slump and labor restless. An Associated Press dispatch reported that government security prices were falling daily, that the purchasing power of the pound had hit an all-time low and that rumors of pound devaluation were floating around London.

Sir Stafford Cripps was telling the people they must submit to a program of austerities. But it was not austerity the people had been promised and they resented it. Clifton Daniel, American news correspondent, reported: "There is not a single Labor Party leader in Britain who will look you in the eye and say that the average man in Britain is better off today than he has ever been." And he added that these leaders know it is the persisting high prices of goods which are eating away Britain's export market—the market that is as essential to her as the gasoline in the fuel tank is to the activity of a motor car. United Press correspondent Hallinan reported that Britain is heading into an industrial crisis and that Cripps had summoned the newsmen to a secret conference and admitted to them that Britain's loss of gold reserves was such that "We may soon be on the spot."

Here is the measure of Socialist failure. Even with Marshall Plan money, Britain is not able to cover the export deficit against her without eating away at her gold. Despite the severity of Cripps' warning in the Commons, Brendan Bracken, Conservative War Information Minister, charged Cripps with failing in his duty in not telling the people bluntly "that England is moving into one of the worst economic crises in her history."

Thus shaken, the Labor Party leaders met at Blackpool in the second week of June, 1949, to formulate their plans for the next election. They were deeply divided about many things. The Prime Minister and his followers were for "slackening the advance." But Aneurin Bevan and his followers were for plunging forward with further socialization. The Socialist cooperative associations, a powerful element in the Socialist ranks, were bitterly opposed to the government's plans for bulk-purchasing— taking over outright the total output of factories and selling it at low prices to the consumers. This they believed would wreck the cooperatives. There was the rash of strikes—the railroad workers who wanted more pay, shorter hours and a hand in management on the syndicalist model. There were widespread demands for higher wages from labor unions in spite of the fact that it is the high cost of production which is devouring Britain's foreign markets.

Almost the first subject forced upon their attention was the question of when to hold a national election. Under the law the date is fixed by the government but must not be later than August, 1950. It may be any time sooner upon a few weeks' notice. When the crisis clouds gathered overhead, Lord Woolton, Conservative Party head, warned that the Laborites might precipitate an election immediately, before the full force of the storm could scatter them. When the Party met, as someone commented, "with Blackpool beneath their feet and black clouds overhead," Lord Strabolgi, Labor peer, spoke up. He was afraid "the country was about to enter into a most difficult situation in which it would be difficult to explain to the people why it had risen and what we had to do. There was a great deal of misunderstanding still and *before the economic blizzard struck us the government should go to the country—this autumn.*" But the leaders insisted properly that the date of the election was a subject for the ministers and besides, there was no point tipping their hand to the Conservatives.

The Party approved the nationalization of cement manufacture, sugar refining, water supply systems, mineral deposits, some sections of the chemical industry, meat distribution, cold storage and industrial insurance. It pledged itself to establish enterprises to compete with private industry and to make bulk purchases to distribute to consumers at low prices.

The leaders appealed to the workers of the nation to put their shoulders to the wheel, to produce more, to enable the nation to export more. But as the conference ended, the Prime Minister hurried from Blackpool to London to deal with the mounting clamor of unions for more pay, better working conditions and a bigger hand in the management of industry. For the approaching slump they reveal they have no plans save to spend more money. Where it is to come from is not known. Certainly it cannot come from America. We cannot go on supporting British socialism indefinitely. The immense sums we have doled out have not been sufficient to keep the Socialist experiment afloat. How much more would we be called on to pay to raise it up when it is sinking?

But a far sterner crisis was upon England. Trouble seemed to be tumbling upon her bedeviled redeemers from every quarter. The causes were simple. Arithmetic and gravity and the laws of physics and nature had caught up with the architects of the Bright New World. Cripps had frightened his Socialist colleagues by telling them that the profit-maker had been liquidated, that there was left no one to pay the bills but the people and that they must produce more or perish. Here was the eminent "Brain" of the party repeating what had been said 30 years before by Rudyard Kipling, the writer most hated by English Socialists. Kipling wrote:

"In the Carboniferous Epoch we were promised abundance
     for all,
By robbing selected Peter to pay for collective Paul;
But, though we had plenty of money, there was nothing our
     money could buy,
And the Gods of the Copybook Headings said: '*If you don't
     work you die.*'"

It was, indeed, the same bleak doctrine announced to the mythical oriental potentate by the solitary economist in his kingdom, who was asked to explain the current depression. He did so in a sentence: "There ain't no such thing as free lunch."

But as Attlee hurried from Blackpool he faced a crisis which was as logical as the bankruptcy petition of the spendthrift. As I have already noted, England cannot produce all the food and industrial raw materials she needs. She must buy these means of life in other countries. She must pay for these imports. She can do this in only two ways—by selling to those countries enough of her own products to balance her purchases or by settling the difference in gold. But she has not been able to sell to other nations enough to balance her purchases. Her principal difficulty has been with her American trade. In the single month of May, 1949, Britain bought from us $151,000,000 worth of goods more than she sold us. She therefore owed us $151,000,000 in gold. She had been running behind in her trade with us on an average of $84,000,000 a month in January, February and March, 1949. In April the deficit made a big jump and in May it soared to twice the average of the first three months. Thus Britain was losing her gold reserves. Cripps had announced earlier that under no circumstances could her gold be allowed to fall below $2,200,000,000. But by June, 1949, it had fallen to $1,630,000,000. If this continued for another six months England would be bankrupt. She stood upon the precipice. And this was the crisis behind the hurried succession of conferences in early July, 1949.

For these disasters, of course, the Socialist engineers had their explanation. It was all due to the depression in the United States which made it impossible for America to continue her purchases in England. Of course, that is not the reason. American correspondents as well as leading British journals have pointed to the reason. It is the high cost of production in Socialist England. British workers will not produce more. They will not work for less. This runs up costs and prices. But this is not all. The nationalized industries are run at a loss. The social services cost billions. These losses and the social insurance costs must be paid for by the government with money raised by taxation. The taxes must be paid out of the incomes of the producers—the owners and the workers. And these incomes are derived only from industry. Industry must put a price on its goods which includes (1) the costs of production, and (2) the taxes to pay government expenses, social service costs and losses on nationalized industries. Hence these vast costs and losses show up in the price of the goods England has to sell abroad. And these prices are so high that England's markets are shrinking. To put it plainly, she is trying to buy *low cost* imports with *high priced* exports. And she just can't make it. Hence she must settle the deficits with her gold and her gold is dwindling. If that is not checked she will sink.

Cripps and his colleagues knew the real cause as well as anyone. That is why Attlee and Cripps and Morrison made frantic appeals to the workers to produce more, to cut costs in order to cut prices. But the workers turned a deaf ear. Great Britain was being swept by an epidemic of strikes—oddly enough, in the nationalized industries. For several months the railway men conducted a Sunday slow-down in protest against a new set of work schedules adopted by the Minister to effect economies. This required many railroad men to be absent from home one night a week and they refused to submit. The slow-down was ended but the union promptly demanded a second pay rise within the year from the government railway management which is losing money every day at the present rates, despite a substantial increase in traffic rates. The coal mines have gone through a series of unofficial strikes, particularly in the large Lancashire fields, about some minor working arrangement. Most serious were the unofficial strikes among the dockers which by July 13, 1949, involved the idleness of 13,000 men and was paralyzing Britain's desperately needed foreign trade. Prime Minister Attlee denounced this as the work of the Communists. But this is not the whole trouble by any means. The Socialist leaders have a commitment to the workers which they have not yet satisfied. They are under contract to deliver to them the Brave New World. During the years they were fighting for power the secret of the Socialists was in the radiant promises of the good life they would bring. Their opponents could never match these promises. They knew what the Socialists are now being told—as if it were a new discovery—that the earth yields nothing save to the labor of man. But the British worker who took these leaders at their word wants shorter hours and more leisure and more food and less taxes. Instead he gets an egg and a half a week, three ounces of butter, six of margarine, one of lard, one of cheese, one of bacon, eight of sugar, six of meat and two of corn beef. And even this thin diet he gets because rich Capitalist America has helped to foot the bill to the tune of billions.

Yet even upon this severe ration the system slowly falls apart. And above the dark forebodings of defeat and failure the eloquent voices of the bedeviled promisers rise, but promising no more, talking no more of the fuller life and days of ease. Now they call for more work and still more austerity. Sir Stafford Cripps asked the workers to "lead dedicated lives." Dedicated lives are for priests and soldiers during war and for ascetics.

Whole populations cannot be asked to lead dedicated lives in time of peace. The workers ask when the dedication is to end and the good life to begin. When will the demands upon them cease and the promises be fulfilled? They are further away now than they were five years ago. In Russia the promisers have been at it over 30 years and all the people have got is ceaseless appeals for sacrifice and dedication.

The dark realities of this floundering regime have brought more than one Socialist up with a jerk. Alfred Edwards, Socialist member of Parliament, declared: "I have spent years discoursing on the defects of the Capitalist system. I do not withdraw those criticisms. But we have seen the two systems side by side. And the man who would still argue for socialism as the means of ridding our society of the defects of capitalism is blind indeed. Socialism just does not work." Naturally he was promptly expelled from the party. Later, in July, 1949, Lord Milverton, Labor Whip in the Lords, created a Labor peer by the party in 1947, renounced his party affiliation during the debate on steel. In a speech on the floor he declared, to quote the London *Times*, that "he had certain aims and ideals and he had thought the Labor Party could 'deliver the goods.' He was now appalled at the type of goods which were being delivered. He thought he was participating in a crusade but found himself a camp-follower in a rake's progress. *The road on which they were traveling led to a precipice at the foot of which clearly emerged the totalitarian state.*"

This is the system of Fabian Socialism we are being asked to imitate.

CHAPTER FOUR

Socialism in America

We have seen what socialism means in England and the plan by which it was brought into effect and the consequences visited upon the English people. Now we are prepared to ask and answer the question: Do we have in America any movement comparable to the Fabian Socialist movement in England? And if so, what is it doing, how is it progressing and what are its chances of success here?

The answer, of course, is that we do have precisely such a movement here, that it is making rapid strides and that, unless it is arrested, and at some very early date, nothing can prevent its extension here on the British model.

In thinking about this subject the reader must be very careful not to confuse the present virile and growing Socialist movement in America with what we have known for so long as the Socialist Party. The Socialist Party in the United States has reached a very low estate in numbers and in growth. I am referring to an entirely different movement led by entirely different men and under wholly different banners.

The popular conception of socialism, as we have seen it in England, is subjected to two grave misconceptions. There are some excessively sensitive persons who brand almost any intervention by the State into the economic system as socialism. On the other hand, there are far more who imagine socialism means the practically complete confiscation by the State of the whole economic apparatus of the nation.

As we have seen in England, *modern socialism means the assumption by the State of the responsibility and authority for the control of the entire economic system.* This does not mean that the State will take over every farm, shop, mine and factory. It means that the State will take over and operate the great basic functions of credit, electric power, fuel, transportation and insurance, including the so-called welfare activities. The rest of the economic system may be kept in private hands to be operated according to plans made by the State and carried out under the supervision and compulsions of vast and numerous government bureaus.

This is the type of socialism with which America is now threatened. And just as it was gradually spread over England by a movement that meticulously avoided calling itself Socialist, so it is being promoted in America by organizations that never pronounce in public the word socialism. They call their system the Planned Economy. That is a fraudulent brand name. It is used to sell socialism to an unsuspecting population. What that cunning label refers to is precisely the same thing that is now in operation in England. It could be called correctly a Planned Socialist Economy, for that is what it is.

We have had a Socialist movement in this country under one name or another for well over 50 years. The Socialist Party we now know as such was organized in 1901 by Eugene V. Debs, who ran for President as its first candidate. In 1928 Norman Thomas, who had joined the Party in 1917, became its candidate for President and he has been renominated every four years since. The Party, however, never became a serious threat here. Debs got nearly a million votes in 1920 and Norman Thomas got 884,781 in 1932. But after that its following dwindled away until in 1936 its national vote was only 187,000. It has had a number of able leaders. Norman Thomas, in particular, has won a unique place for himself in the good opinion of the American people because of his courage, his complete honesty and his great power on the platform as a champion not merely of the Socialist philosophy but of many fine human causes. At one time it had built a considerable propaganda machine. It had the People's House in New York with its large Socialist library and the Rand School which was the center of its educational activity. But it was an honest movement run by honest men who offered socialism to the people and called it by its true name. But Americans made it plain they did not want that. In England the old Fabians, as we have seen, never offered socialism as such. They peddled one product at a time, always omitting the Socialist label. They called their party the Labor Party. And it is a curious phenomenon of our times that at the very moment when the market for the whole range of Socialist merchandise became most receptive in this country, the Social- ist Party in the United States almost went out of business.

This odd effect was due to the fact that a new Socialist enter- prise entered the market. It took over Fabian socialism as its product, but it found a new and attractive brand name for its goods. It was called the Planned Economy. The term "Planned Economy" was a stroke of genius. Certainly at this time every- body agreed that our American system was in a state of dislo- cation and in desperate need of repair. This, we were told, was because it was a disorderly and unplanned system. How ob- vious! What it needed above everything else was some intelli- gent planning. Who could make an intelligent objection to planning? The very name almost disarmed its critics.

Of course there could be no reason against making plans to revive what had always been known as the American sys- tem, that is, the system of private ownership called capitalism, within the framework of a free republican society. But this is not what the advocates of planning meant. They meant in a general sense that the economic system must *cease to be a free system and that the State, which under our system was forbid- den to intervene in the management of industry, should now be established as the master of industry with the power to make the plans for the whole economic system and for each part of it.*

More specifically, what they had in mind very clearly was that the State should assert its right to own any part of the sys- tem outright or to intervene and control the owners accordingly as the State saw fit. In other words, their specific objective was to socialize the economic system—"the democratization of eco- nomic power" as they called it. Attaining this "democratiza- tion," as Professor Laski said, did not mean "the necessity of taking over all industry and agriculture by the State. Rather,

I think, it means that the *fundamental basis of economic power shall be in the hands of the community*." And he points out that the fundamental bases are the ownership and control of land, state control of import and export trade, state ownership and control of transport, fuel and power and coal and, of course "controls which would operate over those which remain in private hands."

This is precisely what the Economic Planners had in mind and this is precisely what the Fabian Socialists aimed at and succeeded in producing in England.

What do they mean by planning? The central idea in the minds of all the Planners is a great National Economic Board, as Mr. George Soule calls it, or a PPB—Peace Production Board —as Mr. Walter Reuther calls it, or a National Planning Commission as others call it.

The plan has been fully outlined by Mr. Soule in his book "A Planned Society." The Board, he tells us, would make a study of all the problems in all industries. Having done this in any given industry, the Board would then go to the owners and lay down the law as follows:

The Board would make them understand that their enterprise was an obstacle to prosperity and must be reorganized to pay higher wages and sell at lower prices. "We are instructed by Congress to aid you in formulating a plan for these purposes," explains Mr. Soule. "We are delegating our experts to aid you at every stage of your researches. We will give you two years to produce a proposal. . . . When it is ready we will approve or disapprove it. . . . If you do not produce a plan . . . that we can approve, we are instructed by Congress to make one of our own."

Then, of course, after the plan has been put into motion the government Planners would keep in close touch with it "to see that the objectives are approached, and in order to correlate the annual plans for wages, employment, production, profits, prices and investment with those of other industries." [1]

[1] "A Planned Society" by George Soule, Macmillan, 1932.

Obviously this Board could not correlate the wages, prices, policies, etc., of this business with the remainder of American industry without treating the rest of industry to the same dose. Mr. Soule faces the possibility that the problem in any given industry might defy solution under private industry. The Board might attempt a solution by large-scale cartels or compel consolidations under public regulation. But it might find itself forced to impose complete public ownership by a "publicly owned corporation which would buy out the existing individual owners with debentures." Mr. Soule makes it plain that this Board would approach its problem without any bias in favor of either public or private ownership. It would choose the form best suited to the individual problem. But he adds, with charming naïveté, that in the case he selected for illustration, as in other basic industries, he would suggest public ownership.

Mr. Reuther, the head of the United Automobile Workers union and now one of the most powerful figures in American labor politics, has some ideas on how this would work in the automobile industry. Mr. Reuther and his economic consultants believe that the automobile industry should be planned. At present, the General Motors Corporation, for instance, makes the most elaborate plans for operating the General Motors Corporation. This Mr. Reuther thinks is sheer nonsense. The automobile industry must be planned as a whole and these plans must be made not by the managers of the automobile industry but by representatives of management, representatives of labor and the agents of the State. This group, in which management would of course be a minority of one, would then study the whole industry, determine how many automobiles ought to be made and what types—that is, for what income groups—and how many each producer would make, what prices would be charged, what wages would be paid to labor, what hours labor would work, what management would get and what investors would get and, as part of the department of compulsion, what priorities in steel and other materials each producer would get and then, of course, over all this would be the power of the government alone to see that the plans were carried out.

This is planning for the automobile industry. But there would be similar planning councils in every industry, all of these councils being responsible to the great central Peace Production Board or National Planning Council, which would be empowered to alter the plans in order to make them fit into the plans made for all the other industries. This is what they have in England now and this is what we shall have in America if the ideas of the Economic Planners go into effect.

A somewhat more detailed list has been set up by Mr. Stuart Chase.[2] Mr. Chase, who is always the honest disputant, gives an outline of the things which would either have to be established or considered:

1. There would have to be a "strong, centralized government."

2. The powers of the President would have to be enlarged at the expense of the Congress and the courts.

3. The government would have to control banking, credit and security exchanges.

4. The government would have to guarantee employment, if not through private industry, then through armaments and public works.

5. Of course there would be old-age pensions, mothers' pensions, unemployment insurance, etc.

6. The government would have to insure to all "food, housing and medical care."

7. There would have to be support of these operations with government funds obtained by borrowing if necessary.

8. A managed currency.

9. Complete control by the government over foreign trade.

10. Control of natural energy sources such as hydroelectric power, coal and gas, transportation and agricultural production.

11. Recognition of the necessity for subjecting labor unions in so extensively controlled an economy to government control to the "point of prohibiting strikes."

12. Youth camps for young men and women. At this point

2 "The Road We Are Travelling" by Stuart Chase, 20th Century Fund, 1942.

Mr. Chase suggests that these would be devoted to "health, discipline, community service and *ideological teaching consistent with those of the authorities*." Mr. Chase does not indicate that he endorses this, but that this is one of the things we would have to face.

13. Heavy taxation.

14. There would not be so much "taking over all industries in the old Socialistic sense." The government would set up controls without ownership. Mr. Chase, who is one of the most intelligent and intellectually honest of all these Planners, at this point pulls away a little from deciding whether this whole list is good or bad. He admits these are clearly contrary to the liberal democratic ideal but he insists "there is not an item on the list which is not applicable in some degree to the United States." And he says that all of these items are points to be considered in the new structure which is being molded and that the names by which it will be called—socialism, state capitalism, fascism—mean nothing. The essential content is the important point.

Mr. Chase does not say so and perhaps would not agree, but what they add up to is British Fabian Socialism and American National Socialist Planning, which are precisely the same under different names. The most extensive care is observed to get away from the word "socialism." This is the advice George Bernard Shaw[3] gave the English. He admitted the English could not nationalize everything. He believed it more likely that nationalization would become the rule and private enterprise the exception. And he urged that we stop talking nonsense about socialism and set to work to nationalizing various things and make an end of insisting on what it shall be called. "And I," he adds, "who said 40 years ago that we should have had socialism already but for the Socialists, am quite willing to drop the name, if dropping it will help me to get the thing done." This is the shrewd counsel which the American new-style Socialists have adopted. They have dropped the name socialism.

[3] "The Intelligent Woman's Guide to Socialism and Capitalism" by George Bernard Shaw, Garden City, 1928.

This, then, is the Socialist program for America. It envisions:

1. The taking over by the federal government, in time, of all the enterprises controlling credit, power, transportation, coal and steel, the complete federal control of our export and import trade, and the assumption by the federal government of all insurance functions.

2. The subjection of what remains in private enterprise to federal planning on the model described, and

3. The assumption by the federal government of complete responsibility for the continuous functioning of the whole economic system at or near full-scale operation and adequate provision for the whole population of jobs or such arrangements in the way of pensions or other payments in case of old age, widowhood, orphanage, unemployment. Included in this, of course, will be the socialization of medicine.

This is the plan which constitutes the chief and great menace to our freedom and to the good life in America, because under this now fairly well defined type of socialism there can be no freedom and there will be no abundance, as I will presently show. This is the great menace, *not the communism of Russia nor the Communists in America.*

I do not mean that the communism of Russia is a thing to be brushed aside. But there is nobody in America, including the Communist Party, trying to force Russian communism on America now. The Communist Party here, far more intelligent about its objectives than we are about ours, knows that America is not ripe for the Russian form of communism. The American Communist Party works for three objectives:

1. It seeks to wreck our existing economic system and to discredit our political system.

2. It promotes all sorts of Fabian Socialist planning enterprises because it believes that we can be induced to embrace these and it knows that these will spell the ruin of our own system.

3. It seeks to promote whatever may be the immediate objective of the Russian government at any time.

So far as our foreign affairs are concerned this Party is an aggregation of traitors, providing espionage for an alien government and carrying out the orders of that government. So far as our purely domestic affairs are concerned you will find its members teaming up with various little groups of Fabian Socialists in all sorts of enterprises designed to push us along the road of Fabian socialism on the British model, which the Communist knows is not a terminus but merely the first stopping place of the journey. The Communist, in our domestic affairs, is a menace to the extent that he is the partner—and often a very effective partner—of the Fabian Socialist.

The real enemy we must identify and fight at every crossroad and at all points is the American edition of the British Fabian Socialist, who is engaged in a sneak attack here as his comrades were in England, who denies that he is a Socialist and who operates behind a mask which he calls National Planning.

Not long ago, a collection of European Communists, including a number of Russians, were amongst us attending a Cultural and Scientific Conference for World Peace. There was much ado about it and some very angry voices were raised at the presence of these enemies of our civilization on our soil. And loudest among the protesting voices were a number of gentlemen in an organization called Americans for Intellectual Freedom. But the ringleaders in that organization are the men who must be identified as infinitely more dangerous to the civilization of this country than the small group of Red birds of passage against whom they were fulminating. For it is they who are plotting to wipe out the traditional political and economic civilization of this country and to supplant it with a system of organized social life on the Fabian model. They wrap themselves in a mantle they call anti-communism. But they are pro-Socialist. They are not willing, of course, publicly to concede that. They are Planners. That is, they are Socialist Planners—and unless they are identified, recognized for what they are and are stopped *they will destroy this country.*

This movement began to assume ominous proportions around 1938. In that year the old depression of 1929 raised its terrifying head again. Eleven million people were out of work. The

Democratic Party, which was certainly not a Socialist party, had no more medicine to prescribe. The administration had spent 20 billion dollars to prime the pump and again the pump refused to work at more than a lazy gait. There had been, of course, a great deal of talk about planning. But the word had not yet got into vogue in its Socialist sense. Moreover the theory of planning had lacked one vital ingredient. The vagaries of the money economy still remained a puzzle, even to the Planners.

It was at this point that a group of men headed by Dr. Alvin Hansen appeared in Washington with an American edition of Mr. John Maynard Keynes' theories of spending and national debt. All the government planning involved government spending. And that involved heavy taxation and debt. Taxes and debt were supposed to be an evil and were certainly unpopular. But now came the new theory that governments could borrow almost indefinitely, that government borrowing was a good thing, that government debt was not a burden, did not have to be paid and was, literally, an unmixed blessing. A whole batch of Harvard and other professors vouched for the soundness of this thoroughly cockeyed theory. Planning, now equipped with the new engine of government borrowing, took on a new and vital form. And the whole brood of Socialists and Technocrats and Fabians swarmed into Washington.

I need not enter here into any account of the circumstances which made it possible for them to move into almost all the important bureaucratic posts during the war. The fact is that they did. It is also a fact that this second World War did for us something very much like that ominous job which the first World War did for England—though the injury was by no means so grievous. It has, however, produced a number of dislocations affecting the very essential parts of our whole social system.

There is, however, nothing in all this in the least disturbing to our National Socialist Planners. They believe that the depression and then the war, along with the devices introduced into our system by the New Deal, have effectually wrecked the American Capitalist system. They have looked upon the performances they were able to promote during the war and the results they have obtained since the armistice as complete proof not merely of the soundness of their theories but of the inevitableness of their dreamed-of revolution. They believe that they have America trapped within the walls of their economic theories. It may be that they are right about this. I do not, however, believe it to be true. But I do believe that only a tremendous and heroic effort can extricate us. Across the ocean they see what our blind politicians refuse to see—that Socialist parties are everywhere operating the crippled and limping Capitalist societies of the Continent and that England, the birthplace of capitalism and the free society, has fallen utterly into the hands of the Socialist leaders of Britain. America, they confidently believe, is next on Karl Marx's list.

To sum this all up, we are now facing a new drive, such as was made in England, to put this country into the Socialist camp. It is being carried out precisely as it was in England. The product on sale is Fabian Socialism and this means the taking over, one at a time, of the great basic functions of credit, power, transportation, steel and basic metals, and the submission of the rest of the system to National Socialist Planning at the hands of the federal government.

In this system a network of bureaus armed with oppressive authority will swarm over the whole apparatus of the private sector of the system and exhausting taxes will drain to the dregs the profits of this sector to support the ever-expanding socialized sector. The operation of this sort of society will force the most fundamental alterations in our political system, because it must be obvious to the most casual student that the American political system is utterly unsuited to such a society.

All this will be accomplished by the same strategic plans that proved so successful in England. And now we must turn to observe the steps by which this is being accomplished here, how far it has already proceeded and what remains to be done. But first, I am sure the reader is asking himself—who are *they*? Who are these mysterious American Fabians? What is their organization and who are their leaders?

CHAPTER FIVE

The American Fabians

THERE WAS until recently no general staff of a Fabian movement in America that could be compared to the Fabian Society of England. The development of the movement here did not progress in the same sequence as in England. The crash of 1933 and the inauguration of Franklin D. Roosevelt brought into Washington swarms of men and women with blueprints for the reconstruction of civilization upon every conceivable model. Such a miscellaneous menagerie of social philosophers was never before gathered together in one distracted neighborhood. They disagreed with each other upon every conceivable postulate of policy.

But in time the left-wingers, for reasons we need not examine here, began to float to the top. Because of the presence in positions of power of men like Wallace, Frankfurter and Tugwell, streams of out-of-work or low-salaried Socialist professors and instructors, young lawyers and economists flowed into positions around the administrative heads of nearly all the bureaus in Washington. As the bureaus increased in numbers, still fresh hordes of Socialist doctrinaires, ranging from dark red revolutionaries to mild-mannered pink conversationalist reformers, multiplied in the government.

But there was no organized group. Little coteries drew together here and there but it was no more than that. It was not until around 1938 that a pattern began to appear. The crackup of 1938, the rise in unemployment, the defeat of so many New Deal schemes, some of them actually reactionary and others quite radical, created the atmosphere and the climate for the new type of European radical as distinguished from the old honest Socialist or Communist. He called himself an Economic Planner.

We now began to see this new form of hooded socialism gaining immense ground. It had a wondrous quality. A man could espouse it without confessing himself a Socialist. Actually a great many of the men who were arguing for the Planned Economy were loudly declaring their purpose was to save capitalism. It was capitalism's last chance. If those stupid blockheads down in Wall Street tossed this chance over, one was told in an ominous whisper, then they were done for.

Meantime, in the 1936 election the Congress of Industrial Organizations had demonstrated the political power of labor and Sidney Hillman was looming up as a challenging force. It was around Henry Wallace at first that this numerous swarm of Socialist Planners gathered. But soon Hillman moved into the picture. Hillman, of course, was a man of sharp and energetic intelligence in contrast to the loose and cloudy mind of Wallace. Besides, Hillman had now ranged behind himself a potent, well-heeled and numerous army of workers.

Meantime, the theory of Economic Planning which Stuart Chase and George Soule had been preaching for a number of years rose up into a kind of welcome respectability. And this philosophy, newly equipped with Alvin Hansen's glorious spending theories and his magical proposals about practically endless borrowing, brought the whole school of planning into official favor. From this point on—even all through the war—this theory became the rallying point for every kind of left-winger, including the Communists who knew it wouldn't work save for a brief interval but who recognized it as a magnificent type of novitiate for the Russian brand of socialism.

The first attempt to provide this idea with an organized propaganda machine was the formation of the CIO Political Action Committee by Sidney Hillman in the 1944 campaign. In this Committee, Socialists of every description—Planners as well as Communists by the thousands—were collected together. To reach various elements outside of labor, Hillman formed at the same time the National Citizens Political Action Committee.

Hillman headed this and it included a hodgepodge of every kind of Socialist left-winger from shell pink to the most flaming flamingo. Another collection of intellectuals was formed into the Independent Citizens Committee of the Arts, Sciences and Professions and this included an imposing list of professors, writers of every description, dramatists, actors, movie stars, lawyers, doctors and editors, almost all deeply implicated one way or another in the great radical war for the Brave New World of the Future.

The Communists were all right in those happy days. No one questioned their honesty, their nobility of purpose, their love of democracy. Russia was one of the "democratic" nations, one of the "peace-loving" nations, even one of the "like-minded" nations. (I say no one challenged the Communists in those days. The Committee on Un-American Activities challenged them but was subjected to the most continuous and angry abuse ever heaped on a legislative body.)

But after Roosevelt's death and the end of the war and after Russia began to insist on enjoying all the gracious gifts which had been made to her by Mr. Roosevelt in eastern Europe and Manchuria, matters changed. Philip Murray and Walter Reuther and others who had been arm-in-arm with the Communists in the Political Action Committees now began denouncing their old comrades. Truman was in the White House, and early in the game he kicked Henry Wallace out of the Department of Commerce and the cabinet. Wallace uttered a war yell, formed the Progressive Citizens of America to succeed the National Citizens Political Action Committee and announced he would form a third party. This fractured the beautiful friendship between the Russian Reds and the Fabian Reds.

The next stage in this eventful history was the formation of the Americans for Democratic Action in January, 1947. This organization has now become the spearhead and the central planning and propaganda machine of the National Socialist Economic Planners in this country. Of course they do not adopt such a title and, above all, they carefully avoid the use of the word socialism. In fact they seem determined to go the British

Fabians one better in their sneak techniques by holding themselves out as the instrument for saving capitalism.

The basis of their whole program is set out in their statement of policy dated March 2, 1948. They make it clear that there are areas of the economy which cannot be controlled while in private hands. These may be dealt with in two ways. One is to have them taken over by cooperatives operating under one of the government agencies—the Rural Electrification Administration, for instance. The other is full public ownership. The balance of the economic system they will subject to national economic planning.

They propose first, of course, a vigorous use of the power to tax and spend to shape and control the economic system. Beyond that they advocate what they call "balanced production targets for the whole economy." There must at once be a use of "price, allocation, inventory and credit controls."

There must be "bold long range programs for the development of our resources, rebuilding of our cities, elimination of our slums and provision for full and equal opportunity for health, education and security"—by the federal government of course. These are trade words with these gentlemen. They are a highly verbose costume of words for socialism. What they intend to bring here is precisely what the Fabians have brought to England.

A pet evasion of this school is to point out that even in England what has been built is not socialism. Only 25 per cent of England's economic system, we are assured, has been socialized, and the remaining 75 per cent is still in private hands. Even the ordinarily candid economist Barbara Ward [1] attempts to pull the wool over the eyes of the American reader by claiming that Britain's economy is only 25 per cent socialized. What England has done is to nationalize all the great essential functions of a modern economic society—power, materials, credit, transport—without which the remainder could not operate at all. It is like socializing the engine in the automobile, and still calling it a 75

[1] "The Acid Test of the Welfare State" by Barbara Ward, New York Times Magazine, March 20, 1949.

per cent Capitalist machine. Miss Ward neglects to point out that in addition to operating these basic industries the Socialist government controls all the rest under the system of Economic Planning, which is as radical a principle as outright nationalization. Harold Laski has explained very clearly that possession of these great basic services—credit, power and transportation—makes the planning for the remainder and the enforcement of the plans far simpler. The private operator who resists compliance with the plans made for him can be compelled to obey by the threat of having his gas, electricity, coal, credit and transportation cut off.

Americans for Democratic Action have brought together many of the most powerful figures in the three great labor groups—David Dubinsky of the American Federation of Labor, Walter Reuther and James B. Carey of the Congress of Industrial Organizations (CIO), and A. F. Whitney of the Railroad Brotherhoods. There, of course, will be found most of the old New Deal Planners—Elmer Davis, Leon Henderson, Chester Bowles, Wilson Wyatt, Senator Hubert H. Humphrey of Minnesota, who is now national chairman of ADA succeeding Leon Henderson, Paul Porter, Reinhold Niebuhr, young Franklin D. Roosevelt, Lauchlin Currie, Professor Seymour Harris of Harvard, Robert Nathan and a host of others.

The ADA announces that it "is not a political party itself," that it "works through established parties" and that "its tools are education and political action." It declares its intention of "telling the people the facts and what they can do about them; working in party primaries to nominate liberal candidates; campaigning for their election." It boasts that it has spread through 48 states with over 75 full-fledged chapters, in addition to 100 student groups. Far more interesting is its statement in a folder entitled "Stop Talking to Yourself" that *"Outstanding is ADA's success in bringing together the national leaders of labor's forces —the AFL, the CIO and the great independent unions. Through ADA they are for the first time united with each other, and with other liberals."*

Of course it will offer, as in England, all varieties of personal benefits to various groups. At the moment it is putting its power behind two very important drives—socialized medicine and so-called civil rights. The real meaning of the latter we shall see in a later chapter. But it will never use the word socialism. That word will not emerge until the country is carried so far along the road that it can no longer be disguised.

Up to now this organization has been working through the Democratic Party, save in New York where it has an outfit of its own. But this phase of the story we shall examine separately.

It may be that the men and women who guide this movement will fail to measure up to the task they have set themselves. But this much is clear. They have taken their place on the battlefield which was occupied in England by the Fabians. They have before them the rich experience of the British Fabians. And they do not lack plenty of advice from some of the very active philosophers of that movement.

CHAPTER SIX

A Note on Communism

AT EVERY STAGE of this subject the Communist issue arises to confuse us. The Communist Party in the United States is a political organization. But it is not a party in the sense in which we understand that term. It no longer puts up candidates for office under its own name. It is, in fact, a secret, conspiratorial brotherhood, engaged in a highly planned program to wreck the American system as a prelude to making this country into a Socialist nation. Equally important, it is the agent of a foreign power in carrying out the objectives of the Russian government in this country. To this extent it is organized treason.

If we consider the Communist both inside and outside the party, it is not a simple matter to distinguish him from the Socialist. He is in fact a Socialist. And as we look over a large collection of people in a New York left-wing gathering, for instance, it would be very difficult to determine at what point any given person ceases to be a Communist and becomes a Socialist or vice versa. If we leave out the purely Russian ingredient, they are all Socialists. They all believe that the Capitalist system must go. They all believe it cannot be ended here overnight, and that, as Lloyd George said, they would execute it, Chinese fashion, in sections. They all believe in the public absorption of railways, electric and gas utilities, mines, banks, and in socialized medicine. They all believe that in time the area of Socialist seizure must be extended. And they all believe that in the meantime the privately owned sector must be brought under national planning and control.

They will differ as to the time table, as to which sectors will be attacked first, and as to the extent to which outright nationalization must go. But they are agreed that socialism in one form or another we must have, and on this plane all of them—Planners and Socialists and Communists—are the same. They are Socialists in fact, and must be grouped together as enemies of our traditional American system.

The Communist Party members, however, are far more aggressive and truculent. They believe in direct as well as in political action. They are not strong enough here to start a revolution by means of violence. But they believe in those strategic and tactical devices, outside of purely political action, which will most swiftly bring about the collapse of our traditional political and economic structures. They support any legal or extra-legal action that will tend to wreck the private enterprise system.

For instance, the Communists, who are much more realistic than their softer Socialist comrades, know that nothing will wreck the Capitalist system more quickly and more surely than extravagant spending and the accumulation of public debt. They are therefore for any plan or program that will tend to pile on top of our creaking Capitalist vehicle new tons of debt. Our less intelligent, and often stupid and mushy Socialist reformers who frequently know little economics and despise its dull and dreary lessons, support public spending because its effects are immediately pleasant and they have been persuaded by a new school of economists that it is a perfectly sound policy for a private enterprise system.

The Communist Party seeks by artfully and very intelligently planned programs to create as much discord and disorder in our social system as possible. For instance, it has created innumerable organizations—Communist-front organizations—which bear attractive and humanitarian names, ostensibly set up to promote the interests of some racial, regional or class group but actually to arouse them, to make them angry, to stir up divisions and hatred among these groups. The Communists' business—and they go about it systematically and intelligently—is to set off Negro against white man, Catholic against Protestant and both against the Jew and the Jew against both, to inflame worker against his boss and the boss against the worker, North against

South, East against West, town against country, and various American groups of foreign origin against each other. There is a devilish cunning in this, and I know it is very difficult for the average American to believe it.

It is this terrible fact which for so many years the Committee on Un-American Activities has spent so much patient effort bringing to public attention. For this the members were subjected to a steady stream of abuse such as has been showered upon no other public servants. Despite some false starts and some unhappy errors their work stands today as a monument to their vision and their patriotism. They have compiled a list [1] of 1160 organizations and movements brought into existence by the American Communist Party to promote all sorts of seemingly laudable social objectives. The list is available to any student who wishes to consult it in the published reports of the Committee. These organizations were formed to invade every class in the community—workers, farmers, Negroes, racial and religious groups of every description, political and welfare groups of all sorts. Thousands of citizens who were not Communists were induced to lend their names to these seemingly proper social causes and millions of dollars were contributed by innocent dupes to finance them. The injury that has been done and continues to be done is beyond measure.

Until the war ended, you would find in these innumerable front organizations the names of most of those men and women who have been prominent in Socialist and planning activities. They were just Socialists together, pursuing a common aim—differing, of course, here and there in methods and distance. They had one absolutely common objective—the destruction of the system of private enterprise and our traditional political system. It must be said in justice that the one Socialist group that held aloof from these Communist marauders, attacked them, sought to expose them and were in turn smeared and traduced

[1] Special Committee on Un-American Activities, House of Representatives, 78th Congress, 2nd Session: Appendix IX (in six sections with cumulative index) on "Communist-Front Organizations." U. S. Government Printing Office, Washington, 1944.

by them were our old-time democratic Socialists led by Norman Thomas. And it is this Socialist faction which has been almost exterminated by them.

On the contrary, you will find a man like Dr. Frank P. Graham, long-time president of the University of North Carolina and now in the United States Senate, not merely an innocent victim in one or two such Communist-front organizations, but a member of eighteen different movements and causes organized and promoted and run by the Communists, before the war, during the war and since. You will find him the active head of one of the most sinister of these Communist-front organizations, publicly denounced as such and admitted by the Communists to be such. Does this mean that Dr. Graham is a Communist? Does it mean that he is a tool of the Communists in knowingly promoting some traitorous enterprise of Communist Russia? Not necessarily. It does mean that in these numerous activities he and the Communists were marching in the same direction on our domestic battlefront. It means that he was *en rapport* with them in their purely American objectives.

Dr. Graham is no fool. He is extolled as one who did this because he is a lover of freedom. What companions for a lover of freedom! The simple truth is that Dr. Graham is a National Socialist Planner, that he is an active part of the drive that is being made to push this country along the road of British Fabian socialism. But Dr. Graham does not carry the Socialist label around on his lapel. The governor of North Carolina has recently appointed Dr. Graham to the United States Senate. Of course the governor would never dream of appointing Norman Thomas, if he were a North Carolinian, to the Senate, because Norman Thomas says openly and frankly, "I am a Socialist," and he declares openly he will have no truck with American Communists, whom he believes to be enemies of human freedom. But the governor feels no hesitation in appointing a hooded Socialist like Graham who is up to his neck in Communists but manages to conceal his Socialist identity from an uncritical Southern governor by this fraudulent label of Economic Planning.

My object in these comments is to point out that as we look around for the men and groups who are promoting the assault on the American system of political and economic life, there is no need to make too fine a point of the distinction between Communists and Socialists and particularly between the Communists and the Socialist Planners. Up to the end of the war the Communists and the Planners were all good soldiers together, marching shoulder to shoulder in the great cause of wrecking the American Capitalist society in favor of the brave new world of socialism. They penetrated labor unions, professional groups, teacher organizations, political bodies, religious bodies, racial groups. They did their great job together—Planners and Communists—upon the minds of the American people. They helped to create the mood of frustration and despair about our traditional civilization.

Together they painted a picture of America which made this country seem to be rotten with poverty and injustice, crumbling away under the greed of a handful of exploiting "malefactors of great wealth"—"one-third of a nation ill-fed, ill-housed and ill-clothed"—cruel discrimination dividing us into sheep and goats, Negroes hanging from southern tree limbs, tubercular children and starving sharecroppers pining away in horror, the frontier gone, the age of invention over, no prospect before us but to follow the great "democracies" of Europe and throw ourselves into the arms of the Planners.

Since the war ended and the terrible truth about Communist Russia now stands stark before our eyes, the name "Communist" has become highly unpopular. It is now popular to be a Red-hunter. All our noble labor leaders and writers and dramatists and newspaper editors and political leaders are busy hanging "anti-Communist" streamers about their shoulders. It is now the mode to be anti-Communist. And behind that anti-Communist label you can be a Socialist or a Socialist Planner or anything you choose. The Communist himself long basked in security behind a similar streamer. He called himself an anti-Fascist. But he was still a Communist and a Socialist. Now the Socialist Planners call themselves anti-Communists. But they are still Socialists or Socialist Planners. Also they call themselves liberals. But let us not be deceived by the names under which they operate. They are Socialist Planners, which means they are Fabian Socialists. And as we look around for the real enemy who must be kept constantly in sight and kept ruthlessly out of positions of power where they can do their work of destruction, we need be in no doubt about that enemy. He is the Socialist Planner.

CHAPTER SEVEN

The Capture of the Unions

THE OLD TRADITIONAL Socialist Party in America never made much headway with the labor unions. The Socialist label was the chief reason. More important, however, was the fact that the American Federation of Labor under Samuel Gompers held to the original British concept of the union—a collective bargaining instrument for the workers to represent them in their relationships with their employers. And Gompers, like his early British mentors, rigorously kept the unions free from partisan politics. In England this policy was broken down, as we have seen, as part of the Socialist plan to capture the official machinery of the unions not merely for political purposes but for revolutionary purposes. It was broken down here in 1936.

But the initial steps originated inside the unions themselves. John L. Lewis, Sidney Hillman and David Dubinsky did this job in a deal with President Roosevelt. They put their unions and the whole CIO, which they organized, into politics and gave Roosevelt $500,000 for his campaign fund in return for certain pledges from him, chiefly concerned with the Wagner Labor Relations Act. It was much like the deal between the trade unions and the Liberal Party in England in 1905 in which the unions supported Asquith and Lloyd George in return for a repeal of the Taff-Vale decision.

One of the by-products of this alliance was the delivery of the unions into the hands of the Socialists. What these radical labor politicians wanted was the officers, the funds, the educational machinery of the unions. And this propaganda apparatus they proceeded to use upon their own members. The members of the unions take little part in union affairs. They expect their leaders to fight for them for higher pay, shorter hours, better working conditions. If the leaders do this job energetically and successfully the members are satisfied. The leaders have been able to bring to bear upon the minds of their members a vigorous propaganda pressure for all sorts of other blessings which are to come, not from the bosses, but from a benevolent government. Old-age pensions and more old-age pensions, unemployment insurance and, in general, a government officialdom which operates on the side of labor in all labor disputes and a government policy which includes all sorts of guarantees of perpetual employment, endless prosperity and government responsibility for the welfare of every working man. None of these things is called socialism. They are not all necessarily socialism. But they are what might be called the first steps in a Socialist program, after which follow such things as socialized medicine, TVAs by the dozen and endless government spending to provide endless employment at constantly rising wages.

How far the union leaders who are now for the most part committed to the Socialist program of the Socialist Planners can carry their memberships remains unknown. One thing, however, is certain and that is that the immense, powerful, well-financed propaganda apparatus of the unions is now at the service of the Socialist Planners.

An immense amount of newspaper space has been devoted to supporting the charge that many unions have been dominated by the Communists. The charges were practically all true, particularly in the CIO, of which Sidney Hillman was the head until his death, when he was succeeded by Philip Murray. John L. Lewis said, February 29, 1944, "Philip Murray is today the prisoner of the Communists in his own union. They control him and the CIO through their seats on his executive committe. And there isn't a blessed thing he can do about it."

On the executive board of the CIO at the time there were the following labor leaders with notorious Communist affiliation records: Lewis Alan Berne, Donald Henderson, Joseph P. Selly, Julius Emspak, Grant W. Oakes, Eleanor Nelson, Joseph F. Jurich, Ben Gold, Morris Muster, Harry R. Bridges, Ferdinand

C. Smith, Lewis Merrill, Abram Flaxer, Michael J. Quill, Joseph Curran, Reid Robinson, E. F. Burke, Frank R. McGrath.[1] There were others, these being the most flagrant instances.

When Earl Browder was jailed and a petition to release him was presented to the President, the names of 513 labor leaders in the CIO were on the petition. And when in January, 1944, the *Daily Worker,* the official daily organ of the Communist Party and the most abusive and violent Communist publication on this continent, celebrated its 20th anniversary, 144 CIO leaders saluted it in a congratulatory document. These labor leaders represented 25 out of the 39 international unions affiliated with the CIO.[2]

In 1946 William Green declared: "We don't have any Communism in the American Federation of Labor." It is true that there was less of it there than in the CIO, but some AFL unions were heavily infiltrated and influenced by industrious Communist elements. For instance, Local 644 of the West Coast Painters was headed by Herbert F. Sorrell, a notorious Communist fellow-traveler. In order to extend its sway in the movie industry it chartered as locals the Screen Story Analysts, the Screen Cartoonists, and the Screen Publicists. There were plenty of Communists in the Hotel and Restaurant Employees International Alliance and the Bartenders International League, in the Bakery and Confectionery Workers Union, in the Actors Equity Association and in the International Typographical Union. In the latter two they formed only an aggressive minority.[3]

However, let us not be confused by this whole subject of Communist union infiltration and control. The fact of the matter is that the great mass of labor unions are Socialist controlled and a part of these Socialist-controlled unions are of the Communist variety.

[1] "Report on the CIO Political Action Committee," House Committee on Un-American Activities, Mar. 29, 1944 (78th Cong., 2nd Sess.).
[2] *Ibid.*
[3] "Communist Power in United States Industry" by Andrew Avery; reprint of series of articles, Jan. 13 to Jan. 31, 1947, in the Chicago *Journal of Commerce.*

There was always a good deal of argument as to whether Sidney Hillman was a Communist. Certainly Hillman had played ball on a large scale with the Russian Communists. But one thing is clear, and that is that Hillman was a Socialist. There was never any question about that, and his union was wholly Socialist controlled. We look upon David Dubinsky as a doughty foe of the Communists in the unions. But David Dubinsky, whose union is one of the most important in the AFL, is a Socialist and his union is a Socialist union.

At intervals we hear of some violent upheaval in this or that union in which the Communists are thrown out of power. Back in 1938 there was such a row in the Maritime Union. Its paper, the *Pilot*, had been an active champion of communism. There was a "progressive" revolt, the "progressives" won and the Communists were put out of power. But the new officers and the entire office staff were composed of Socialists.

The Communist label is getting to be a costly handicap now. Labor leaders, and others, who basked happily in the sun of Communist favor and support are running away from the Communist brand, and in many unions the Communists are being thrown out. As each new Communist victim is heaved from his union office the event is hailed as a great victory for "our side" —for the American way—for democracy—and various other causes including "liberalism." Of course it is proper to dethrone these Communist union leaders. But let us restrain a little the exuberance of our rejoicing.

An excellent example of this confused thinking is the praise that was showered on Mr. Walter Reuther, the brave young champion of "democracy" who in 1946 defeated the Communists' forces in the United Automobile Workers union led by R. J. Thomas. This powerful union has about a million members. But what has happened now is that Reuther, the Socialist Planner, has displaced Thomas, the Communist fellow-traveler, and the union has been brought more neatly into the orbit of the Socialist Planners. How far Reuther is to the left it is not easy to say. Back in 1934 he and his brother, Victor, went to Russia, where they got jobs in a Russian factory in Gorki. While they were there, Detroit was torn by strikes and the boys wrote home to friends. Here is a part of one of the letters:

"The daily inspiration that is ours as we work side by side with our Russian comrades in our factory, the thought that we will forever end the exploitation of man by man, the thought that what we are building will be for the benefit and enjoyment of the working class, not only of Russia but of the entire world, is the compensation we receive for our temporary absence from the struggle in the United States. And let no one tell you that we are not on the road to socialism in the Soviet Union. Let no one say that the workers of the Union of Soviet Socialist Republics are not on the road to security, enlightenment and happiness."

He was transported with admiration of what he saw in Russia:

"In our factory which is the largest and most modern in Europe, and we have seen them all, there are no pictures of Fords and Rockefellers and Mellon. No such parasites, but rather huge pictures of Lenin. Red banners with slogans 'Workers of the World Unite' are draped across the craneways. . . . We are witnessing and experiencing great things in the U.S.S.R. . . . We are watching daily, socialism being taken down from the books on the shelves and put into actual application. Who would not be inspired by such events?" [4]

Walter Reuther saw communism in action in Russia and he liked it. Of course what he saw was socialism and that was what he liked. I do not for an instant imply that Reuther is now a Communist in the sense that he is a supporter of the Soviet government in all its harsh and aggressive international policies. Doubtless the whole of Russian policy, the wider area of the Russian European program did not operate upon his mind. But the pure socialism which he saw in one sector of that Red world filled him with enthusiasm. He is older now and he is ambitious. He is still a Socialist. But he is a National Socialist Planner. And this does not include any immediate nationalization of the auto-

[4] "What Does Walter Reuther Want?" by Jack Alexander, *Saturday Evening Post*, August 14, 1948.

mobile industry. His union wants the government to build and operate some steel plants, which would be a fair beginning on the Fabian model. But an industry like the automobile industry, thus far, is to be assigned to the State *planned* area of the economy rather than the State *owned* part.

Reuther, as I have already explained, and his advisers believe that there is only one way to avoid the succession of "booms and busts" for the automobile industry and that is by Planning. Planning means submitting the entire industry to a Socialist Planned Economy.

One large question rises to confront us at this point. How many people will be willing to invest money in an industry run on this plan and crushed under taxes like those which bleed white the British auto manufacturer? How many executives would be willing to operate under such a regime? Of course the most informed Socialist students know that this sort of operation is impossible and that it will be only a matter of time when the State would be called on to take the next step and take over the industry outright.

Yet this is the pattern for American industry, aside from those basic enterprises that will be taken over outright. A pamphlet issued by David Dubinsky's International Ladies Garment Workers Union declares that "The history of the ILGWU has demonstrated that the workers can be entrusted with the task of running industry in the interest not only of the working class but of society in general far better than the present masters of industry who, blinded by profit, would rush on to suicidal death."[5] The program of the Socialist Planners is to transfer the more basic industries to the State as proprietor, to commit the remainder to planning by management and labor under State chairmanship and supervision and to make the State responsible for the continuous operation of the entire system and for the security and welfare of every individual.

It is these Socialist Planners who are now in control of the American labor unions and, as I have indicated in a preceding

[5] "The Story of the ILGWU," New York, 1935.

chapter, we find the leaders of these unions part of the political engine known as Americans for Democratic Action which is expected to sit at the center of this Fabian revolution, guide its destinies and bring all the elements of popular support together.

Their immediate drive is for socialized medicine and public housing. The housing industry for low-income citizens having been wiped out by the government by means of a confiscatory tax system and by the building unions and their "conscious withdrawal of efficiency," the job is now declared to be one for the State. It is a simple matter to Mr. Walter Reuther, who is dangerous because he is an effective speaker and a good political organizer, and also because all the great problems seem simple to him. He demands now nothing less than twenty million houses for workers in the next ten years. It is merely necessary to convert the aircraft plants to assembly line manufacture of houses, which will sell for $6000. This huge number of houses would result in new communities requiring new shops, new roads, new movie theatres, etc. The houses would cost 120 billion dollars; the community improvements another 120 billion. It would all be managed and financed by the government, because it is "too big a job for private industry." It is all so simple. One part of this trick not explained is how Mr. Reuther would bypass the power of the building construction labor unions with a plan like this, which dispenses with their services.

Of course, like our pundits in Americans for Democratic Action, these labor men shy away from the word socialism. In the case of some of them it is downright ignorance. Others understand fully that they are deceiving the people. Recently a group of these Socialist Planners published a book outlining their doctrines and their hopes. These correspond precisely with British socialism. But they have called the book "Saving American Capitalism." Philip Murray indignantly denied the charge of a business man that his program was "nakedly socialistic." "We want the free enterprise system to really work for all Americans," he insisted. The error in the business man's criticism was that it is "nakedly" socialistic. It is far from naked. It is all dressed up in the most colorful capitalistic silks and laces. Secretary of Labor Tobin has just assured us we have nothing to fear on the score of socialism. They are all trying to save capitalism. Can he really believe that? And if he does, is he sufficiently informed to hold a cabinet portfolio?

The history of British politics from 1905 on is filled with the assurances of men like Lloyd George, Herbert Asquith, Lord Grey and numerous confused labor union leaders that England was in no danger of going Socialist. The reader may recall the reference in a previous chapter to the comforting words of Asquith and Grey, that "we could sleep more safely in our beds" and that "I regard the advent of a Labor government with no apprehension at all" at the very moment when they were installing Socialist Ramsay MacDonald as Prime Minister.

The meaning of all this is that, as in Britain, Fabian Socialists, known here as Socialist Planners, have, as part of their plan, got almost complete possession of the apparatus of the American labor unions. Up to now they have been able to draw along with them to the polls the rank and file of their members. The promise of so many benefits and graces at the hands of the State has been, of course, a powerful inducement to their members to follow their lead. How far they will be able to march the millions of American labor union members behind the Red flag of socialism when the full road is revealed remains to be seen.

Certainly no intelligent effort has been made to counteract this powerful drive with an educational program designed to answer the propaganda of the union Socialist indoctrination machine. There is no evidence that the American workman favors socialism. The test will come when the present artificial boom expires and the nation sinks down, as is inevitable, into a depression. Will the American workman at that point blame the men who have misled him? Or will he harken to the cry that will then go up that the new and deeper troubles are only a final proof that we must have more rather than less socialism?

CHAPTER EIGHT

The Socialist Invasion of the Democratic Party

W<small>E HAVE SEEN</small> how the American labor unions have become a part of the American Socialist Planners' political and propaganda machine, just as the British trade unions came under the control of the British Fabians. The reader will recall that the next important objective of the British Fabians was to penetrate the British Liberal Party. This they did until the Liberal Party, powerless to attain or hold power without the support of the Fabians, became their servant and ultimately perished. We shall now see how this part of the plan has been carried out in America.

The Democratic Party here was the counterpart of the British Liberal Party. It championed, as a rule, the fortunes of the "common people"—in the old phrase—and looked upon Jefferson, the arch-enemy of the all-powerful State, as its founder and saint. If we reread Al Smith's platform in 1928 we will see the traditional issues of the Party reflected there. It demanded that "the constitutional rights of the states be preserved" and it was opposed to "bureaucracy and the multiplication of offices" not because this was extravagant but because it was "*an instrument of State power.*" It called for the revival of local self-government and economy in the administration. It demanded funds to extinguish the national debt, then 16 billion dollars, "because a national debt *discourages initiative and enterprise.*" This was a normal Democratic platform. And four years later when the nation had been assailed by the depression, the platform did not differ in its fundamental approach. Whatever its imperfections or virtues, it was a platform upon which any orthodox Democrat might have stood.

I do not recall all this to chide the Democratic Party with having gone back on its party pledges. There is nothing unique about that. Parties have promised to reduce taxes before and raised them instead. They have demanded tariff cuts and increased them when in power. I wish merely to indicate the wholly orthodox character of the Party's position in both 1928 and 1932. In the past, American political parties have differed about all sorts of policies. But so far as I know there has been no great difference between them about the fundamental nature of the government. No major party has hitherto attempted to alter the structure of either our economic system or our political system upon a revolutionary scale. The unique character of Mr. Roosevelt's policy after 1936 is that he then began a systematic attempt to change the essential structure of our economic system. I do not know how far he realized what he was doing. He was, as always, not choosing a course but yielding to political pressures and expedience.

Any fair-minded observer of the economic dislocations which Mr. Roosevelt faced in 1932 will understand that they presented problems of the greatest magnitude. The flood of laws and experiments that raced across the scene in that first term may be dismissed as little more than the natural consequences of the violent economic crash which afflicted the nation. There were numerous left-wing expedients. But there were as many right-wing measures. Actually the most important political phenomena of the first term were (1) the plunge into the Welfare State and (2) the decision of the labor unions to abandon their historic role and imitate their British brothers by formally entering into politics.

In the second term the upward swing of business under the influence of public spending halted and the President found himself faced with a return of the depression and, by the end of 1938, with more than eleven million people out of work. It was at this point that the next great crucial event of Mr. Roosevelt's domestic adventures took place.

Beginning in 1933 there had poured into Washington a great number of people—mostly young men—who came after a while to form an ideological army under the leadership of a small group of social philosophers who heard in this 1938 recession the first real "death rattle" of the Capitalist system. I do not believe that the public has any conception of the enormous number (thousands of them) of so-called intellectuals—teachers, lawyers, writers, preachers, scientists, professional men of every type—who never before were identified with any radical party or faction but who filtered into all sorts of key positions as economists, counsel, statisticians, engineers, public relations men in the innumerable newly created bureaus. As the depression began to crawl back in 1938, great numbers of these men and women, turning definitely to some radical explanation of our distress and some radical solution of it, found a comfortable haven in this new school of Planners.

This cult of Economic Planning had what socialism did not have in this country. It had respectability. It had the imprimatur of Harvard professors. It had a name which recommended it to the student's mind. It became possible for a young man actually to be a Socialist without adopting the name. Few of these men had any understanding of the history of British socialism at this time. Few realized they were merely falling into the dialectics and forms of British socialism. Present in Washington in positions of high authority were men like Wallace, Tugwell, Hillman, Henderson, Douglas and others who provided the leadership.

The labor movement under Sidney Hillman and David Dubinsky was now up to its neck in politics. And almost without any formal resolutions to this effect, here was a numerous new army of radicals inside the Democratic Party. It was at this point that the counterpart of the British Fabian movement took definite form. And it took form inside the body of the old Democratic Party. Meantime, the great bulk of the old Socialist Party had moved wholesale into the Democratic Party. For instance, in 1932 Norman Thomas got 884,000 votes on the Socialist ticket. But in 1936 he got only 187,000. The combined vote of the Socialists, the Social Labor Party and Communists in 1932 was over a million. In 1936 it was only 280,000. And in 1940 it was cut in half. There had been a mass migration of Socialists and Communists into the Democratic Party. Thus the New Deal wrecked the old Socialist Party. But in good time the old party of Jefferson would find a new Socialist party stirring in its womb, which would one day destroy it altogether.

Politically the Socialist and Communist parties have become unimportant. The struggle for socialism has moved to an entirely different battlefield under a wholly new war plan. Up to now it has carried on its struggle inside the Democratic Party, with the result that the Democratic Party is now at its mercy in precisely the same manner as the British Liberal Party came to be the prisoner of the British Fabian movement. By this I mean that from now henceforward the Democratic Party must comply with the plans and demands of the Socialist Planners who have moved into it with their labor battalions or else go down to defeat. That Party, therefore, cannot elect a candidate for President without the aid of the Socialist Planners and without surrendering to them on all their ideological demands.

It is possible to prove these statements definitively. The American Fabians, like their British comrades, have organized their own party in America. But they have limited this action to the single state of New York. They went no further elsewhere because the swift surrender of the Democratic leaders made it unnecessary. And perhaps the war interrupted any further political stratagems they may have considered. But as the Socialist Planners have their own party in New York it is easier to see what the effect on the Democratic Party is there than in other states where the Socialist Planners cannot be identified so clearly.

The American Labor Party was organized in 1937 by the Socialist Planners. It included, however, many who were not Socialists but who joined merely because they saw in it an instrument to smite Tammany Hall in city affairs. Few of these remain in it now. Now let us see what the effect of this party has been on the Democratic Party in New York State.

Here is the vote of the Republicans and Democrats in the presidential election of 1940 in New York State:

Willkie (Republican)	3,027,478
Roosevelt (Democrat)	2,834,500

If there had been no other votes, Willkie would have carried the state. He got 192,000 more votes on the Republican ticket than Roosevelt got on the Democratic ticket. But Roosevelt, in addition to his nomination by the Democrats, was also nominated by the American Labor Party. And this party gave him 417,000 votes, more than enough to overcome Willkie's lead. Without the votes of the American Labor Party, Roosevelt would have lost the State and its 47 electoral votes.

The same thing happened in 1944. Here was the vote:

Dewey (Republican)	2,987,647
Roosevelt (Democrat)	2,478,598

Thus Dewey had a clear lead of 500,000 Republican votes over Roosevelt's Democratic votes. By this time the American Labor Party had split. In a bitter struggle the Communists took it over, whereupon the Socialist Planners withdrew and formed the Liberal Party. The Communist American Labor Party nominated Roosevelt and he accepted the nomination. The Socialist Planners' Liberal Party also nominated him with his consent. And these two parties together gave him 800,000 votes in New York State, thus overcoming Dewey's Republican lead.

The point I am trying to make clear here is that the Democratic Party in New York State cannot possibly carry an election without the aid of the Socialist votes—the Planners and the Communists combined. The proof of this is abundant. In 1938, Governor Herbert Lehman ran against Thomas E. Dewey for the governorship. Here again Dewey got 300,000 more Republican votes than Lehman got on the Democratic ticket. Lehman had to depend on the 419,000 votes of the Labor Party to win.

Now witness once more how this left-wing group can dictate in New York. Dewey, defeated in 1938, ran again in 1942. By this time Jim Farley had broken with the President and his left-wing friends. The Socialist Planners demanded the nomination of Senator James Mead. Farley balked and named Attorney-General Bennett instead. The Socialist Planners this time, instead of endorsing the Democratic candidate, named Dean Alfange on their American Labor Party ticket. Bennett, thus deprived of the Labor Party votes, lost. The Planners had proved to the Democrats that they can defeat that party whenever it refuses to do their bidding. They demonstrated more. They proved that not all their strength was in the Labor Party. They showed that they had at least 600,000 votes inside the Democratic Party which remained away from the polls in that election.[1]

This left-wing vote in New York remains split. The Communists and their fellow-travelers are in the American Labor Party. The Socialist Planners are in the Liberal Party. In the 1948 election the American Labor Party pulled away from the Democrats and supported Wallace. By doing that they deprived Truman of the electoral vote of New York. Truman got the Democratic votes and the votes of the Liberal Party (Socialist Planners). Here are the figures.

Dewey (Republican)		2,828,764
Truman (Democrat)	2,572,048	
Truman (Liberal)	209,541	
		2,781,589
Dewey's plurality		47,175

But the American Labor Party polled 501,167 votes. This was more than enough to have given Truman the state had the

[1] The line-up of the Socialist Planners in 1942 was not yet too clear to all their supporters. It is quite difficult to make any reliable estimate of their actual strength in New York. We do know, for instance, that they were able to round up 403,000 votes for the Labor Party ticket. But they had undoubtedly a very large number who were not yet prepared to go outside the Democratic Party and continued to vote, if at all, the Democratic ticket. This constituted a very large number which has been constantly growing. However, we do know that in 1942, when the Socialist Planners refused to support Farley's nomination of Bennett on the Democratic ticket 600,000 persons who voted the Democratic ticket in 1938 remained away from the polls. Thus the refusal of the Planners to support Farley's wing of the Party not only deprived it of the 403,000 votes cast for the American Labor Party, but of 600,000 Democratic votes that were not cast at all.

Labor Party chosen to support him, as it did Roosevelt in 1940 and 1944. The results are even more impressive in congressional races in New York City, where, following precisely the British example, the Socialist groups threw their strength to the Democrats in some districts while in other districts the Democrats nominated men satisfactory to the Socialist groups.

The election of young Franklin D. Roosevelt, Jr., to Congress in New York City is a particularly illuminating exhibit. The late Sol Bloom was elected to Congress from that district on the Democratic ticket for many years. In the 1949 special election to fill Bloom's seat, the Democrats refused to nominate young Roosevelt. They named instead Justice Benjamin Shalleck, a highly respected Democrat, whereupon the Liberal Party nominated young Roosevelt, who received an additional nomination by a hastily improvised group called the Four Freedoms Party. In the election which followed Roosevelt got 31,037 votes on the Liberal ticket, while Shalleck got only 24,363 on the regular Democratic ticket. Roosevelt got an additional 10,000 on the so-called Four Freedoms ticket. These Liberal votes can be given to a Democratic candidate or taken away at will by the Socialist Planning leaders.

This Liberal Party is now the political arm of the Americans for Democratic Action in New York State. The Communists have suffered a grave setback everywhere and it is a reasonable prediction that much of the American Labor Party strength will now seek refuge in the Liberal Party.

What is true in New York is also true in Connecticut, New Jersey, Massachusetts, Michigan, Pennsylvania and other northern states, particularly the large industrial states. But in those states the Socialist Planners have not yet gone outside the Democratic Party into a separate organization. Hence their power is not so obvious to the casual citizen. It is there, however, and in all of those states the Democratic Party must now yield to them on policy. It is their prisoner utterly. It is precisely in the same position as was the Liberal Party in England. The Democratic Party now faces the ordeal which the Liberal Party faced from 1905 to 1923. The more it yields to the demands of its relentless Socialist Planners, the more it antagonizes large elements of traditional Democrats. The loss of these is becoming more and more evident and becoming more and more a problem which the Democratic leaders must face, but which the Socialist Planners too must face.

The Socialist Planners have cracked the problem in the North. They can dictate policy to northern Democrats always. But that is not sufficient. They are now face to face with a critical decision. Will they desert the Democratic Party entirely and form a third party? Or will they make the effort to deal with the southern problem within the Democratic Party? Shortly after the 1948 election most of the labor leaders, as well as some of the ranking Planners, announced their intention of forming a third party, a party definitely committed to labor—actually a Socialist party on the British model but concealed behind the label of labor. Later other counsels prevailed.

Now their plans remain in abeyance. It is a political problem of the first magnitude. If they form a third party the Democratic Party in the North would shrink to futility, as the Liberal Party did in Britain. But there is a good deal of hazard in abandoning a machine which they can control in the North in favor of splitting the existing incongruous Democratic hosts into two hostile groups. However, the unnatural union between the southern Democrats and the northern Socialist Democratic machines is at an end. The moment is at hand when a determined effort must be made to crack the Democratic South. That may seem an impossible task to the uninitiated. But it does not look that way to the Planners. They have a strategy for it. They have just fought one battle. But another and far more formidable one looms ahead. In the next chapter we will see their war plans for capturing the South.

CHAPTER NINE

The War on the South

THE COUNTRY has recently witnessed a struggle in the United States Senate around the proposal of the President to put federal force behind the guarantee of what is called "civil rights." Few of those who read of the filibuster conducted by the southern Democratic senators understood the real purpose behind this bill. Ostensibly it was to give to our Negro citizens equality of rights of various kinds with their white brethren. But the real objective was little discussed and even less perceived by the casual newspaper reader.

Of course the problem of the Negro and his position in the South and, for that matter, in the North is a perpetual irritant. It is not easy to square the discriminations against the Negro with a number of the most rapturously repeated phrases in accepted national philosophy. There are some aspects of the question that ought to be kept in mind. First of all, the lurid and sensational stories about lynchings and hatreds and suppressions and oppressions have been outrageously exaggerated. It is a fact that almost all of the publicity about the outrages against Negroes in the South has originated in the propaganda agencies of the Communist trouble-makers. Why is the Communist so deeply stirred about the Negro? Is he trying to correct injustices suffered by the Negro in order to improve his lot here and make him love America more? We know that the Communist has one supreme interest and that is to excite and stimulate the hatreds of every class in the country.

Sooner or later this country must face the problem of the Negro. It is simple enough in New York. It is not so simple in Mississippi, where the Negroes almost equal the whites in number, or in Georgia, where Negroes outnumber whites in probably half the counties of the state. White supremacy is a phrase encrusted with unpleasant connotations in the North. But in hundreds of southern counties where Negroes outnumber whites the people are sure that if the Negroes voted there would be not white supremacy but Negro supremacy. In the light of our professed beliefs about the rights of man, however, it is not an easy matter for many of our people to face up to this problem squarely. It is a fact often overlooked that in the South the Negro has made great progress. And it seems to me I begin to see a glimmer of hope in the possibilities which lie in education for the Negro.

In all the welter of words in type about this problem I have seen very little about the number of schools, high schools, colleges, professional schools in the South. One day an educated Negro population, rather than the poor cornfield worker and the illiterate serving man, will confront the people of the country. Time, education on both sides of the color line, patience, understanding may lead us to a happier relationship. But one thing is certain. This is no spot for the trouble-maker, the revolutionist, the Communist bent on mischief, on division and disturbance.

This problem was thrown into the Senate in 1949 by the President. I have, I believe, made it clear that the President is completely the prisoner of the Socialist Planners among his supporters, who elected him and who could break him pathetically tomorrow if it suited their purpose. It was in obedience to their imperious demand that this question of a hurry-up solution of the Negro problem in the South was hurled into the Senate. Now what was their purpose? Was it love for the Negro? Was it a wish to advance his position? Not at all. The purpose was entirely a part of the effort of these Socialist Planners to solve the great crucial political problem which confronts them. The Negro is merely to be one of the tools in the job.

The Socialist Planners have succeeded in capturing the votes of the Negroes in the North. For years after the Civil War the Republican Party got the votes of northern Negroes. But with the advent of the New Deal and the distress among the northern and southern Negroes and the great streams of relief money at the disposal of the Democratic politicians, the Negro was brought en masse into the Democratic fold. This, however, hardly describes the performance perfectly. The depression and the rise of the Communist and New Deal Socialist wing in New York, with Harry Hopkins sitting at the cashier's window, made it possible for the Socialist wing of the Democratic-Red alliance to capture the Negro votes. Today the Socialist movements have that vote in their bag. And they believe they can do the same thing with the Negroes of the South if they can get the vote for them.

Their program in the South therefore is twofold: (1) To get the vote for the Negroes there, and (2) to round up the Negro voters under the Red banner of the Socialist Planners. They believe the second objective will be simple if they can attain the first. How they will use these Negro votes in the South if they can get them to the polls is yet to be determined. But the possibilities in this for our revolutionary philosophers is tantalizing. The part which Negroes might well play in Southern elections if they have the vote is readily seen from the following figures (1940 Census) of white and Negro population in the southern states:

State	Whites	Negroes
Mississippi	1,106,327	1,074,578
South Carolina	1,084,308	814,164
Alabama	1,849,097	983,290
Louisiana	1,511,739	849,303
Georgia	2,038,278	1,084,927
North Carolina	2,567,635	981,298
Virginia	2,015,583	661,449
Florida	1,381,986	514,198
Arkansas	1,466,084	482,578
Tennessee	2,406,906	508,736
Texas	5,487,545	924,391
Kentucky	2,631,425	214,031
Oklahoma	2,104,228	168,849

Even in those states where the percentages are smallest the radicals believe that the Negro vote could be decisive, along with the poorer white sharecroppers and reinforcements from labor voters in the growing industrial centers. The Socialist Planners believe that the Negro, as the highly dramatized underdog, nursing his ancient grievances against the white population, filled with a sense of wrong, would be easy pickings for the Red agitator. Whether the radical leaders would decide to marshal these votes within the Democratic Party or in a third party is one of the problems with which they are now struggling. But first of all they must get for these vast hordes of Negroes the right to vote. They may do this. But if the Negro permits himself to be used by these revolutionary Planners to attempt the destruction of our institutions, he will probably be the greatest sufferer in the process. All Americans will understand the effort of Negroes to get the vote in the South, but they will not look with complacence on any effort by the Negroes to destroy our institutions in the process.

One would be fatuous indeed were one to dismiss these ambitious plans as impossible. How many thoughtful observers would have believed that the drive to admit the southern Negro to full suffrage would be spearheaded by the Democratic Party and led by a President from a border state? How many would have believed that the Democratic Party in the North would be today so completely in the toils of a Socialist faction? The task these men have set themselves is indeed a difficult one. But it is by no means impossible. For among them are men who are masters of this revolutionary technique, which is literally a closed book to their southern Democratic opponents.

Let me illustrate. I have indicated that there are two prongs to the strategy—the admission of the southern Negroes to the vote and their capture by the Socialist Planning propagandists. I am quite sure there are few people in America—even those who follow these affairs closely—who have any conception of the extent and vigor of the drive to round up the Negro population of the South, and the North as well, for socialism. Much of this has been done by the Communists, who are past masters at this art. But we need not trouble ourselves too much as to whether any particular movement is Communist or Socialist.

The objective is always the same. The radical revolutionary propagandist knows that people must be dealt with on their minority group level, and that even a minority group divides naturally into differing subminorities.

For instance, for dealing with even so small a group in this country as the Finns, the Communists have organized four separate fronts—ostensibly Finnish committees. In the case of the Negroes the Red propagandist knows that they are not all of one mind, do not all think alike and are moved and molded in their thinking by various age, class, economic, social and religious considerations. The left-wingers—mostly the Communists—have brought into existence in the last dozen years a large number of front organizations for imposing their ideologies on the Negro mind. A front organization, of course, is one which presents a more or less respectable and non-suspect façade behind which the revolutionary objective is carried on.

In the case of the Negroes I hesitate to give the number lest the reader believe I am exaggerating. As a matter of fact, these organizations number 87—organized and promoted and in many cases originally financed by Communists or left-wing groups, but having among their directors a number of highly respected persons deceived by the apparent objective, yet utterly ignorant of the real objective. The publicly advertised objective is always to raise the standard of some Negro group—the standard of living or education or social justice. But the real purpose always is to line up the Negroes on the side of the Communists or their near brothers, the Socialist Planners. They thus invite the sympathy and support of great masses of Negroes and accustom them to looking at short range and with a benevolent eye at the radical philosophies wrapped up in the social or charitable or religious or educational programs of the front organization.

There is, so far as I know, no organization anywhere which is countering this mass attack, though there are innumerable organizations in the South doing charitable, educational, social work of the greatest value, but doing it without the political purpose of the Reds. The movement organized by Reds and

Socialist Planners is supported by large funds, an ocean of propaganda, innumerable weekly and monthly journals, speakers, forums, pamphlets, meetings, demonstrations where advisable. It has been going on for years and drawing respectability and prestige from the names of many white citizens, among them people of wealth, college presidents, high-ranking officials, scientists, preachers, journalists, teachers from our great universities, movie and radio stars and public men of the highest eminence, most of them having little knowledge and no understanding of the purposes back of the whole drive.

In the presence of this problem we have to recognize the fact that the Negro question does not stand before us alone. If there were nothing else involved, the position of the true liberal might well be very different. But here he must make a choice. Is he going to put his weight on the side of a revolutionary Red drive to recruit the Negro in order to swell the ranks of the army of Socialist voters who will be used to complete the destruction of our political and economic system? Or will he say that this Negro question must be subordinate to the greater one of preserving our political and economic civilization? Will we hurry the Negro to the polls to set us upon a path which will end in destroying the liberties of us all—white and black alike?

To support my statement of the extent and variety of the drive that has been going on, I give here the names of the organizations formed in the last dozen years to operate upon the minds of our Negro voters which were brought into existence and directed by Communists or Socialists or both, as printed in the reports of the House Committee on Un-American Activities:

African Blood Brotherhood
All-Harlem Youth Conference
All-Southern Negro Youth Congress
American Negro Labor Congress
Association for the Study of Negro Life and History
Atlanta Committee for Defense of Angelo Herndon
Chicago Conference on Race Relations
Chicago Joint Committee Against Racial Discrimination
Colored Community Club

Committee to Establish Youth Centers in Harlem
Committee for Racial and Religious Tolerance
Conference for Constitutional Rights for Negroes
Council on African Affairs
Council of Negro Organizations
Council for Negro Women in America
Council of United Negro Labor Leaders of Washington
Council of Young Southerners
Ethiopian World Federation
Federated Youth Clubs of Harlem
Georgia Fact Finding Committee
Harlem Christian Youth Council
Harlem Church Youth Conference
Harlem Interracial Forum
Harlem Labor Union
Harlem Legislative Conference
Harlem Non-Partisan Committee to Support Supreme Court
    Reform
Harlem Peace League
Herndon Defense Auxiliary Committee
Herndon Petition Committee
Institute of Race Relations
International Committee on African Affairs
International Institute for African Affairs
International Trade Union Committee of Negro Workers
Joint Committee to Aid the Herndon Defense
Langston Hughes Peace Group
League of Struggle for Negro Rights
League of Young Southerners
Marian Anderson Citizens Committee
Miami Negro Youth Council
Michigan Negro Congress
National Association of Colored Women
National Committee to Abolish the Poll Tax
National Conference of Negro Youth
National Council of Negro Women of the United States
National Council of Negro Youth
National Negro Congress
Negro Champion
Negro Commission Bulletin

Negro Cultural Committee
Negro Freedom Rally
Negro Labor Victory Committee
Negro Liberator
Negro People's Committee
Negro People's Theatre
Negro Playwrights, Inc.
Negro Publications Society of America, Inc.
Negro Quarterly
Negro Women, Inc.
Negro Worker
Negro Writers Guild
Negro Youth Congress
Negro Youth Council for Victory and Democracy
Negro Youth Federation
Negro Youth Theatre
New Africa
New South
New York State Conference of Negro Youth
Paul Robeson Peace Group
Permanent Committee for Better Schools in Harlem
Philadelphia National Negro Congress
Scottsboro Defense Committee
Society for Negro Culture
Southern Council for Human Welfare
Southern Committee for People's Rights
Southern Negro Youth Conference
Southern Women's Association for the Prevention of Lynching
Southern Worker
Southern Workers Defense League
Southern Youth Congress
Standing Committee on Negro Welfare
Statement by Negro Leaders Protesting Attacks Against Communist Candidates
Statewide Conference of Negro Youth
Texas Negro People's Wartime Committee
United Aid for People of African Descent
Washington Negro Youth Federation
Westchester Negro Youth Institute
Williamsbridge Scottsboro Action Committee.

CHAPTER TEN

The "Kingdom of God"

MODERN REVOLUTION has its propaganda techniques. The American looks upon himself as a master of advertising and of public relations. But he knows nothing of modern revolutionary propaganda. Its method is an assault upon the minds of the people. Its aim is to plant in the mind a fixed idea, a settled conviction. Once that is done, that idea will condition and shape all the decisions of the man into whose mind it is inserted. For instance, the Communist and Socialist Planners in this country have sold to an enormous number of people one simple idea—that the State owes every man a living, a job if possible, security in the absence of a job. With a man who has accepted that idea, it is useless to argue about taxes, prices, the Constitution, human rights, freedom of speech.

The revolutionary propagandist knows that it is a waste of time to appeal to a whole nation as a unit and on the same plane. People do not think in such vast masses. They think as members of groups—groups formed by racial, religious, economic, social or regional interests. It is for this reason that the Communists— far more intelligent in this field than our American Social Planners who are just beginning to learn the art—have brought into existence so many "front" organizations, each designed to appeal to some class upon its class plane. Remember the eighty-seven separate organizations or causes to deal with every phase of Negro interest and thought.

In promoting certain controlling ideas among various defined groups the Communists know that there are what are called "key minds"—men or women who by reason of their special position in the group are peculiarly effective in planting ideas. Now it would be extremely surprising if so intelligent and skilful a propaganda organization as the Communist or Socialist idea-planters overlooked the churches. I now propose to direct your attention to a condition that will, I believe, startle the reader as much as it startled and shocked me.

I touch upon this phase of my subject with the greatest hesitation. It must be clearly understood that this is not an attack on religion or on any organized church. It has been my own faith that the greatest bulwark against the essentially pagan doctrines and institutions of modern socialism would be the Christian churches. And I still believe that. Yet one cannot put aside lightly the statement of Clement Attlee, the British Socialist Prime Minister, who said of England: "The first place in the influences that built up the Socialist movement (in England) must be given to religion." It is for this reason that I now turn with much reluctance to a condition that has grown up, not in our Christian churches and not in the hearts of our Christian preachers, but in the organization of a clique of Christian ministers and laymen to poison the minds of the Christian churches in America with the principles of radical socialism.

There is an organization known as the Federal Council of Churches of Christ in America. Its constituent members are twenty-five Protestant denominations in America. These denominations claim to represent 142,354 local congregations with a membership of twenty-seven million Christian men and women and youth. This organization is governed by about 450 representatives—delegates from the constituent denominations. But the actual directing body is an executive committee of eighty members.

What the political and social views of these eighty members may be I do not know. But I do know that this powerful Council issues periodicals, pamphlets, books and booklets and sends out preachers to preach the gospel, and that it is by all odds the most powerful apparatus in existence for propaganda among the Christian laity of America. And I know moreover, and assert, that *many of the men most powerful in directing its affairs are using its machinery to promote the interests of a Socialist revolution in America.* The humble communicants of countless thousands of little churches all over this broad land dedicated to the worship of God and the spiritual needs of their people are paying the bills for this propaganda drive. I do not believe that they realize what is being done by these leaders. Now let us look at the facts.

The chairman of the policy committee of the Federal Council of Churches is Bishop G. Bromley Oxnam. He has been the president of the Council and remains the most powerful factor in it. He was a bishop of the Methodist Church in Omaha and Boston and finally in New York. He has been accused of being a Communist and a Communist fellow-traveler. This arises out of his connection with a number of Communist-front organizations.

He was a sponsor of the United States-Soviet Friendship Rallies and was chairman of the Massachusetts Council of American-Soviet Friendship. Following the shocking execution of two Polish Jewish unionists by the Soviets, a Russian delegation was sent here to counteract the unfavorable publicity attendant on this crime. Bishop Oxnam turned up as a member of the reception committee. Far more serious, he was an editorial adviser of a notorious magazine misnamed the *Protestant*, operated by a violent radical named Kenneth Leslie, which, using the Protestant label, carried on the most outspoken, blatant propaganda for communism and the most vitriolic abuse of Christian churches and churchmen that were fighting communism.

Bishop Oxnam was one of the sponsors of a Committee to Aid Spanish Democracy, which was Communist inspired and which was not aiding democracy, for there was no such thing in the Spanish Communist government which was overthrown. He took part in a round table on India of which the chairman was Guy Emery Shipler, a notorious Communist apologist, and whose secretary was Robert Norton, a member of the Communist Party. These were strange companions for a bishop who occupied at the time the presidency of the Federal Council.

Dr. Oxnam is far too intelligent a man to be fooled by these associations. But there is no point in calling him a Communist. He is a Socialist. And he is one of the new school of Socialist

Planners well over to the left of that section. He has exhibited a peculiar and active interest in Russia and in Communist activities. And I would say that this interest is merely an evidence of his interest in socialism.

I have read his books. He takes occasion at times to make some critical observations about Russia. But these are far outweighed by his favorable comments. He tells how he saw young women coming up out of the Moscow subway in their overalls and covered with mud. "But there was a light in their eyes," he exclaims. Wherever he saw them—at the theatre or the opera —they thrilled him. "They were builders," he says, "sharing the culture of a new society, unafraid of hard labor, uninterested in soft leisure." He was thrilled as he saw them marching—tens of thousands—through Red Square. And he asks: "What drives them to such service?" One would suppose the answer to be obvious. But the Doctor's explanation is different: "It is the call of the classless society and the summons of the New Order." It does not occur to him apparently that they march in obedience to an order from the Kremlin.

In February of 1949, Dr. Oxnam was honored by an award from an Episcopal magazine called the *Churchman*. It was given for his "promotion of good will and better understanding among all peoples." The award was presented at a gala dinner at the Hotel Astor in New York City to which a large number of well known persons were invited—and accepted. The *Churchman* is edited by Dr. Guy Emery Shipler, whose Communist affiliations are open and notorious. And as publicity was given to Shipler and his *Churchman* magazine, many of the noted guests began to duck. Some of those who ducked were men who are themselves far to the left, but Shipler, the *Churchman* and Oxnam were a little too much for them. Even Senator Hubert Humphrey, chairman of Americans for Democratic Action, who had been scheduled to speak, found it impossible to be present.

Whenever these clergymen are challenged on their peculiar affinity for the godless and brutal system of Russia they are always able to point to some criticisms they have made of the

Soviet government. The explanation of their state of mind, however, is quite simple. They condemn Russia for omitting God from her civilization. But they are Socialists. They see in Russia the great experiment in socialism. They wish that to succeed but they would like it better if God were included in the program.

One of the prize exhorters of the Federal Council is Dr. E. Stanley Jones. Dr. Jones spent thirty years of his life in India and then returned here to tell American audiences how much he knew about America. He called upon them to follow Christ as the founder and leader of the Socialist movement—though he did not put it quite that baldly. Dr. Jones is sent out periodically by the Federal Council from city to city to preach the glory of Red Christianity. In a sense he is the author of a wholly new pulpit jargon. The prize specimen of this is his use of the phrase "The Kingdom of God."

The "Kingdom of God," according to Dr. Jones, is socialism, but like all his tribe, he never uses that word if he can duck it. The "Kingdom of God" is not some distant settlement in the Elysian fields. It is a land organized according to the ideas of Karl Marx, softened and illuminated by the Bible. It is the fusion of Christ and Marx. The "Kingdom," he says "is a new social order within the individual *and in the collective life.*" The "Kingdom," he tells us, "would be harnessed to the collective good." There would be a "holding of the means of production by all in behalf of all."

Then he gets down to brass tacks. He answers those who fear that life on a "collective scale" cannot be "born again." That is absurd. "Russia," he asserts, "has done it. She has had a new secular birth." And he declares that in ten years Russia will be the most powerful nation in the world. Why, he asks. "Because she has got hold of a higher principle, cooperation, and it is working out in higher results than we can work out of a lower principle, competition."

He admits that communism is anti-God, yet while being anti-God is nearer to God than religions that worship God in spirit and word "but deny him in social progress."

He sums up communism's indictment of America. America

developed political democracy but it stopped there. It did not develop economic democracy and this has negated our political democracy. We have got to change. There are only two ways to do it. One is by communism and the other is by the "Kingdom." And the "Kingdom," he assures us, "has everything that communism has, minus its dogmatic atheism, its class war, its compulsion and denial of liberty, and plus a great deal that communism has not." In other words, we are to have "everything communism has" plus God, and, of course, a softer regime. This is the "Kingdom of God."

Dr. Jones has another theory which is quite interesting. He thinks the war will have destroyed the worst forms of collectivism—fascism and nazism. Two great powers will be left— America and Russia. "America represents individualism at its best and Russia represents collectivism at its best." He feels a great conflict between these two systems would be a world calamity. They must get together and make "the world cooperative man." He explains that "We would give Russia the first commandment: Thou shalt love the Lord thy God. And they will give us the second: Thou shalt love thy neighbor as thyself." Our individualism and Russia's collectivism will be synthesized to produce the perfect "cooperative man" in the "Kingdom of God." And Dr. Jones is talking with the complete approval of the leaders of the Federal Council when he exclaims: "If you want the Christian Church to help produce that man, *then we are at your disposal.*" [1]

Do the 142,000 Christian congregations know about this offer? Do the twenty-seven million Christian Americans in these churches know about this offer? And do they know that a huge, well-heeled church apparatus using their prestige and their funds is actually engaged in promoting an economic Socialist revolution in this country now?

Of course I would not spend so much time on Dr. Jones were it not for the fact that he is one of the foremost pulpit and platform orators sponsored by the Federal Council of Churches,

[1] "The Choice Before Us" (1937) and "The Christ of the American Road" (1944) by E. Stanley Jones, Abingdon-Cokesbury Press.

and he goes around from church to church spreading this peculiar gospel. Do you think these churches would permit Vishinsky or Molotov to get into their pulpits? Do you think they would finance Earl Browder or W. Z. Foster? Do you believe they would permit Americans for Democratic Action or the Socialist Party of America to occupy their pulpits and their platforms at church expense and under church auspices to preach a Socialist revolution? Obviously not. However, none of these men would be effective because they would come with their masks off. But here is a Christian preacher who has found a new name for socialism—the "Kingdom of God"—and who under the auspices of the greatest religious lay body in America and in the language of the scriptures and with Christ at the center of his appeal insinuates into their minds and hearts the revolutionary doctrines of European socialism.

Dr. J. Henry Carpenter is the executive secretary of the Brooklyn Federation of Churches. He is the author of a book entitled "Peace Through Cooperation." He declares that "Capitalism as we have known it is irreconcilable with an organized society motivated by a spirit of love." And furthermore "Democracy," says Dr. Carpenter, "is the counterpart or even the twin of capitalism." Then he comforts us with the assurance that "The marriage lasted well over 100 years. But the New Deal finally brought it to a finish. And the divorce brought capitalism and government face to face as antagonists. There is not the slightest chance of their ever arranging an amicable settlement." [2]

Both Dr. Carpenter and Dr. John C. Bennett are associated with the Federal Council of Churches. Dr. Bennett, who is chairman of the Congregational Christian Council for Social Action and whose books are widely distributed by the Federal Council, in one of his volumes [3] makes clear that the emphasis in his book is upon "Communism as a promise of a more just order of society and upon communism as a corrective of the attitudes of the conventional Church, while not implying that

[2] "Peace Through Cooperation" by J. Henry Carpenter, Harper & Bros.
[3] "Christianity and Communism" by John C. Bennett, Association Press, 1948.

it is any less important to resist the extension of communism." So far as this has any meaning at all it is "double talk." Dr. Bennett thinks that the "whole Communist attack upon Capitalist society is ethical through and through" and he believes "there is more in common between Christianity and communism than appears on the surface."

The church in America, according to these men, must be made the instrument for bringing about a social revolution. Dr. Bennett makes a profound confession. It is "that the rank and file of Christians, still in considerable measure represent the conventional assumptions of their nation or class but what has happened is that the *change in thought and commitment on the part of those who exercise leadership* has been so marked that the churches are moving in a new direction." Here is an admission that these leaders are running away with the machinery of the churches of Christ without the knowledge or approval of the faithful.

The whole philosophy of this group, which has seized upon the machinery of the churches to preach social revolution, is very clearly set out by Dr. Bennett when he cautions church people to distinguish very carefully between the opposition of Christians to communism because of its irreligion and the opposition of those who are against its economic theories. A great deal of the "propaganda against communism," he tells us, is "controlled by the determination to preserve existing capitalistic institutions. *Christianity has no stake in the survival of capitalism.*"

He points out what I have already stressed in this book, that western Europe is no longer interested in capitalism but in a Socialist world, and one of the reasons, he tells us, that many Christians in western Europe look with dread upon "the thrust of American capitalism into Europe" is because they are "convinced that any economic system that is viable for them must be socialistic." [4]

Nothing done in Russia has shocked the sensibilities of Christians more than that mass dedication of millions of Russian

[4] *Ibid.*

peasants to starvation, many in concentration camps, many in their own fields in sight of their own crops, because they refused to comply with the plans for communal farming. But this does not seem to shock our American church Socialist. Dr. Oxnam, the Christian bishop, says that if the Russian peasant "is a conscientious objector to collective farming there, he suffers as a conscientious objector to collective killing suffers here." [5] Dr. Oxnam is implying that what Russia did to the kulaks is no worse than what we did to the conscientious objectors. They were both noncooperators. One cannot suppress a twinge of horror at this complacent judgment by a Christian minister upon one of the most appalling crimes of history.

These sentiments must not be taken as merely the opinions of isolated individuals. They are from men highest in the hierarchy. There is no one more powerful in the Federal Council than Bishop Oxnam. However, these men have managed to put the Council itself on record. The Council adopted its Social Creed in 1932. Under these carefully selected phrases the real meaning is there for those who wish to use this Creed in their economic evangelism. It reads in part:

"The principle of competition appears to be nothing more than a partially conventionalized embodiment of primeval selfishness . . . the supremacy of the motive of self-interest. . . . The Christian conscience can be satisfied with nothing less than the complete substitution of motives of mutual helpfulness and goodwill for the motive of private gain." [6]

This, of course, cannot be taken as the impractical idealism of a group of zealous Christians who think the world should dissolve in a warm flood of selflessness. The American system of production and distribution is and must be carried on for "gain," which means "profit." And these economic revolutionists in clerical garb know perfectly that they are thus advocating the abolition of our present system of production for profit and the substitution of "production for use" which is

[5] "Preaching in a Revolutionary Age," by G. Bromley Oxnam, Abingdon-Cokesbury Press, 1944.
[6] "The Rise of the Tyrant" by Carl McIntire, Christian Beacon Press, 1945.

another one of the numerous fancy names invented for socialism. This they have put in the Creed of the churches. Yet they
admit the rank and file of their people do not accept it.

This Creed reads like the platform of the Socialist Party. It
is for "subordination of the profit-motive to the creative and
cooperative spirit." It is for "Social planning and control of the
credit and monetary systems and the economic processes for
the common good." It is for socialized medicine, which it calls
"Social insurance against sickness." It is for a "cooperative
world order." [7] And if a congregation is interested in turning
the church into a socio-political unit in the community, one
need but write to the Council and it will receive a little pamphlet by its former industrial secretary, Dr. James Myers, which
will instruct the church in how to organize for this purpose,
including suggestions as to when the church ought to go out
on the picket line and how to picket.

In January, 1945, the Council adopted the following:

> "The right of private property is not an absolute right, but
> a right qualified by the public interest. Likewise freedom of en-
> terprise does not imply absolute freedom but operation of enter-
> prise consonant with the interest of the public and the welfare
> of the nation. . . . We must ask our people to recognize that
> in order to supply these needs for all, *many changes may be
> necessary in our economic practices. These changes will prob-
> ably lie in the direction of a larger measure of social planning
> and control than characterized our pre-war system."* [8]

Here, of course, these men are making an artful play upon
words. The right of property is absolutely essential to the existence of the Capitalist system. No one claims that it is absolute in the sense that a man can make any use he wishes of his
property regardless of his neighbors and the public. Also as to
private enterprise, every Capitalist society finds it essential to
make certain regulations touching the use of property to pre-

---

[7] "Social Ideals of the Churches" (as passed by the Quadrennial Meeting of
the Federal Council of Churches at Indianapolis, December 8, 1932; Abridged
edition, 1942), Federal Council of Churches of Christ in America, New York.
[8] "The Rise of the Tyrant" (italics added).

vent the abuse of a right which is essential to the system. By cunningly twisting these concepts, the Council proceeded to indicate, not that certain additional regulations were needed, but that "there must be changes in our *economic practices*" and that these must be "in the direction of *a larger measure of social control.*" What they mean by social control is made perfectly clear in the statement adopted in 1932 at the time of the promulgation of the Creed already referred to:

> "Industrial democracy is a goal comparable to that of political democracy. . . . In one stage of development cooperation through collective agreements between the representatives of management and of workers, counciled by technical experts may be the most advantageous. Even in this most elementary form of industrial relations the right of workers to organize and to be represented by counsel or agents of their own free choice must be recognized as fundamental. *In another stage, participation of workers in management may be possible and desirable; in another workers might provide their own capital and assume full responsibility; in still another the government might assume and exercise the powers of ownership, control and management for the common good.*" [9]

In our system we say to a man: "Our society recognizes your right to own property. This is the very basis of our economic system. There are, however, certain things you will not be permitted to do with that property—uses which will injure the health, the safety or the rights which other men have to own property." Our anti-trust law is an example. But this new creed does not limit itself to telling the property owner or business owner what he must *not do* in the interest of the public health and other public rights. It proposes what it euphemistically calls "social controls" and "industrial democracy" (which everyone knows is a synonym for socialism) by which it means that the State will not only tell a man what he may *not do* with his property, but will tell him, where deemed necessary, what he *must do* with it, and in certain other cases, will put over him a public official to see that he runs his business according to the

[9] *Ibid.*

plans made by the government and in other cases will declare the State in as a partner and in still others actually take the business away from him and put it under State ownership and operation.

In order to arouse the least amount of suspicion among that vast membership from which it draws its funds and its prestige, this group of revolutionary churchmen adopts these weasel-worded resolutions. They dare not come out openly and adopt a resolution saying precisely what they mean, namely "Resolved that the Federal Council of Churches hereby calls on the people to adopt a form of socialism on the model of England —*as a beginning*."

One delegate to the 1945 conference was the editor of the Muskegon (Mich.) *Chronicle*. He wrote in his paper that the statement adopted by the conference was irrelevant to the subject of the conference and "was dragged in by the heels" and, he added, "it is the kind of resolution that is being constantly lugged in by the heels wherever conferences of churchmen are brought together, and have been permitted to go unchallenged, usually because there was nobody present to challenge them or nobody wanted to make himself personally obnoxious." This delegate then offered an amendment as follows:

> "While the growing complexity of modern civilization has increased the area in which private property is affected by public interest so that the rights of private ownership have been circumscribed by the conceded superiority of the claims of the public welfare, we shall at our peril lose sight of the fact that human liberty has, in every age of the world, found its major expression in recognition of the right of the individual citizen to the fruits of his own toil, energy, ability and initiative.

> "Freedom of individual initiative in the economic realm goes hand in hand with human freedom in the political realm. The two are inseparable." [10]

The president of the Federal Council, Bishop G. Bromley Oxnam, objected to this and it was referred at his insistence to a drafting committee and there buried.

[10] *Ibid.*

Later this editor, in an editorial about this conference, wrote: "To the professional leadership of organized religion in America, taken by and large, with notable exceptions, has been sold the socialistic fallacy with magnificent thoroughness. There is a sort of holy enthusiasm for the cause." [11]

The publications of the Council and its organization are used in numerous ways to promote these economic theories of the men who manage it. And they understand quite thoroughly the value of promoting one idea at a time upon the Fabian model. As first one and then another issue inserts itself into the public consciousness, either through some effort of the Socialist Planners in Congress or in other forms of popular promotion, the Council will be found on the job.

For instance, at the present time socialized medicine, masquerading under the name of medical "insurance," has been selected by the Socialist Planners for an intensive drive. The *Lessons for Intermediates* (a publication for use in Sunday Schools) for April, May and June, 1948, takes up the cudgels for socialized medicine. Article Five of the Social Creed of the Federal Council demands socialized medicine. The *Lessons for Intermediates* is issued quarterly by the Methodist Church, which is controlled by the men who are foremost in control of the Federal Council and the case for socialized medicine is thus cleverly pressed upon the minds of young people in the Sunday Schools—coming not from the Socialist Party, not from the politicians in Americans for Democratic Action, nor from the Communist Party, but from a supposedly purely religious magazine issued by a supposedly religious church organization.

Another publication issued for the Sunday School student is *Classmate*. In the issue of July, 1947, is a touching little story about Josef Stalin by Jerome Davis—of all people—who has a fellow-traveler record as long as your arm. He tells the kiddies in the Sunday School classes, "It would be an error to consider the Soviet leader a willful man who believes in forcing his ideas on others." He is pictured as a noble and tenderhearted man, puritanical and selfless. "No doubt," says Davis, "he has his

[11] *Ibid.*

faults. But can we go out to serve God and the common people of America as sincerely and courageously as Stalin did for what he believed was best for his people? Let us devote our lives to the unfinished task of making America a country with a serving church, a serving state, and a serving economic order."

Fortunately, the existence of this bold seizure of the instrumentalities of our Christian churches has been noted by men within the churches. Large numbers of clergymen have discovered that the pulpit, the Sunday School, the church publications and the secular apparatus of the churches have been slyly confiscated by the Socialist Planning preachers and used not so much to save men's souls as to destroy the political and economic institutions of America. Some years ago a small group of clergymen broke away from the Federal Council of Churches, denounced its methods and formed the American Council of Christian Churches, which is opposed to the Planners' church raid. It now has in its framework representatives of fifteen Protestant denominations representing 3000 separate congregations in organized church groups and an additional 3000 in unaffiliated church units, with a combined membership of 1,500,-000 in every state in the Union. It is growing rapidly. Its president is Dr. W. O. H. Garman of Wilkinsburg, Pa.

The Federal Council of Churches took the lead in uniting a large group of churches in Europe, Asia and Africa to do on the world stage what the Oxnams, the Joneses and the Bennetts have been doing in America. This organization came into being at Amsterdam in August, 1948, as the World Council of Churches, and Bishop Oxnam was named one of its presidents, representing the Western Hemisphere. Opposition broke out to this in Amsterdam where, during the same month, an International Council of Christian Churches was formed, representing Protestant denominations in twenty-nine countries. The Reverend Carl McIntire, of Collingswood, N. J., was named president. This much, therefore, must be said—that the battle within the churches is not going by default.

CHAPTER ELEVEN
War Upon the Mind

THE BRITISH FABIAN SOCIALISTS, like their Continental comrades, in their warfare upon the existing institutions fought on many fronts. But they recognized the fundamental importance of steeping the minds of the masses and particularly of the growing generation in the philosophy of socialism. This great enterprise was carried on not as a debate between thinkers but rather in the form of a war upon established ideas. And this war consisted in taking over, as far as possible, the instruments of communication and of opinion in the nation. The American Socialists have been doing precisely the same thing.

In the preceding chapter I have sought to give an example of this in the case of the churches. I selected that because it is the least known of these enterprises in revolutionary indoctrination. It is, however, only one example. The same determined effort has been made to get the use of the radio, the press, the editorial sanctums of book publishing houses, of the periodical press, of the labor unions and, of course, most important of all, of the secondary schools and colleges. How they use these instrumentalities of propaganda is now becoming familiar to those responsible for them. For instance, only recently authorities in college administration, led by General Eisenhower, president of Columbia and Dr. Conant, president of Harvard, have declared emphatically against the use of Communist teachers in the colleges. It was high time. But it is a mistake to suppose that the Communist teacher is the only menace.

The Communist is banned on the ground that he is disloyal and will use his place on a faculty to promote Russian objectives. The Communist can be very dangerous in a government post where he may have access to government secrets. But this is not true in a college. The only harm he can do there is to promote the Socialist philosophy. This is precisely what the Socialist professor can do—with infinitely more effect because we have given him a coat of approval as an anti-Communist. However, it is important that our people should understand the extent of the Communist and Socialist invasion in our colleges.

In a recent study of this subject, the University of Chicago was shown to have on its faculties 60 persons who were members of various Communist-front organizations. One of these professors was a member of 12 Communist fronts. Another was a member of 14—all organized by the Communist Party. All promote the interests of Communist Russia in America. Harvard turned up with 76 faculty members in these Red front organizations. One of them had joined 23 such "leagues" and "councils". He is a teacher of history. What kind of history does he teach? Is he a teacher or a propagandist? There was another Harvard professor who was in 38 such Communist fronts.

One of these front organizations was called the Joint Anti-Fascist Refugee Committee. On its directorate were professors from Harvard, Boston University, Massachusetts Institute of Technology, Yale, Princeton, New York University, Stanford, Brown, University of California and others. When Gerhart Eisler was indicted this committee raised $6000 for him.

Communists have their own schools. They have a right to have them. One is the Jefferson School for Social Science in New York. Another is the Samuel Adams School in Boston. You will find on their faculties men and women who were also on the faculties of Harvard, Boston University, Smith College and New York University. In the Jefferson and Samuel Adams schools these teachers are not so dangerous. They are properly labeled and they teach students who go to these schools to learn to be Communists. But in Harvard and Smith they are not labeled and they get a crack at the minds of young men and women who are there to be educated and not indoctrinated in Communist or Socialist revolutionary philosophy. The Attorney General of the United States publicly branded the Jefferson and

Samuel Adams schools as Communist institutions. Promptly 313 persons signed a protest petition against this. Of these, 124 were educators. There were 21 from Harvard, 11 from Yale, and various numbers from Princeton, Columbia, M.I.T., and New York University.

What is true of the faculties is also true of the publishing world which supplies textbooks and college literature. A favorite roosting place for these revolutionary gentlemen is in the editorial sanctums of textbook publishing houses. A man has a right to produce a textbook with a Socialist or Communist angle. A publisher has a right to publish it. And he has a right to get it used in schools if he can. But does not the public have a right to call attention to this, to guard against subjecting the minds of students to the influence of textbooks which attempt to sneak into their minds these revolutionary philosophies? From the outcry raised whenever this subject is called to public attention you might suppose that freedom of speech was guaranteed to the writers of Red textbooks but that the same freedom of criticism in some way is denied to citizens who call attention to what they are saying and writing.

This subject is a large one and I have been able here to do no more than direct attention to it as part of the problem of understanding what has happened to the American mind in the last fifteen years.

At the bottom of it is a complete perversion of the whole purpose of the college. Its primary purpose is to *educate* its students. And what its faculty needs is a wisely selected group of competent *educators*—not political propagandists. It is almost inevitable that a teacher of history who is a Socialist—of whatever type—will be subject to that mental affection which assails all thoughtful men who espouse revolutionary ideals, good or bad. Some "noble" impatience boils up in them. They are seized by a hot dedication to the "cause". The Socialist or Communist is a man in arms. Recently, an excellent exhibit of this appeared in the morning papers. Russian astronomers have decided that our knowledge of affairs "beyond our galaxy" which means, I take it, on the other side of the Milky Way, should be enlarged.

In convention assembled, the Socialist astronomers decided that they must intensify their work in the "regions beyond the galaxy," which would be a very proper enterprise for astronomers, to be approached with some degree of humility considering the distance and vagueness of the starry world they wish to explore. But this they must do, they inform us, "to counterbalance bourgeois cosmology." They proclaim "that it is necessary to expose tirelessly this astronomical idealism." And they pledged themselves to "fight relentlessly" against "cosmopolitan formalism" and particularly against the "reactionary-idealistic theory of a finite widening of the universe." This, of course, is a perfect example of the mental attitude of the revolutionary propagandist, rather than of the scholar. You will find your Socialist professor—Russian, British or American—ever eager "to make war" on something or other. He is not an educator. He is a social warrior. And he can be depended upon to use his place in the classroom to promote these revolutionary objectives.

But this is not the whole of it. He does not fight alone. Having got a foothold in a faculty he is tireless in using his position not merely to bring in new recruits from among his Socialist brothers-in-arms but in keeping out those who disagree with him. He uses his position in the faculty to promote organized Socialist enterprises and to instruct and urge the students who fall under his influence how to get possession of the opinion-making posts in the student body. And we must not overlook the fact that his own post in the college gives him a prestige which he uses and which the Socialist or Communist groups outside the college use with deadly effect to promote their several plans.

Often these Socialist propagandists refrain from openly promoting socialism as such. They promote Socialist objectives. And almost never do they admit that they are Socialists. They are willing to be known as Economic Planners, a mask which seems to offer them complete protection. These Socialist objectives are almost invariably, inside the colleges, the same as the so-called Communist objectives. They are of two sorts: (1) One includes an incessant attack upon the essential elements of the American system, in order to break down the faith of students in our institutions; (2) the other is to promote some specific policy which will have the effect of advancing their Socialist dream. In a Socialist State there would be a great number of separate activities. One would be State direction of banking policy. Another would be State ownership of power. Still another would be State ownership of transportation. Another would be socialized medicine and so on. No one of these alone would amount to socialism. But all of them together do make a Socialist State. Hence these gentlemen inside the schools can use their posts to promote each of the separate Socialist enterprises in turn, while disavowing the label of Socialist. To this end they twist history, they distort economic statistics and theory in the classrooms and on the lecture platform. They work incessantly to bring to the campus thinkers of their own stripe and to object, sometimes frantically, to those who disagree with them, while protesting vigorously their own special right to freedom of speech.

Indeed, it is this last point on which most stress should be laid. The whole so-called intellectual world has been subjected for a generation to this persistent and relentless pressure to push into places of influence in schools, in magazines, in the editorial offices of newspapers and particularly in the critical departments of the press—literary, theatrical and musical—those who form part of this pink intelligentsia. In short, this is not a mere matter of "free speech" in the intellectual world. The Socialist part of it has turned it into a war—a war to get possession of the pulpit, the editorial page, the radio microphone, the movie screen, the book publishing editorial office and the research departments of the government. It is a war in which they assert for themselves the right to push and haul and traduce and exclude their rival intellectuals while demanding for themselves the extremest limits of freedom. It is war, and those who believe in our institutions and who are opposed to pushing this country down the dark road followed by Russia or Britain or Germany or Italy must accept the gauge of battle and pursue their own objectives accordingly.

Mr. Arthur Krock, a careful and even cautious commentator

in the New York *Times* upon the passing show in Washington, has offered some observations on this worth heeding. He points out that in the last 16 years "the growing testimony of the press, the letters to the editor columns, the radio, book reviews, and other media for carrying persuasion to the people . . . is currently from the left." He comments that theorists of the New Deal and the Fair Deal "comprise a large number of handy college historians and law professors." He indicates that "another important element in this change is the increase in the number of syndicated writers from Washington of the leftist persuasion." [1]

This has not happened by chance. It is the result of constant pressure by the highly excited Socialist warriors in schools and press and public life and the flabby indifference of their opponents who are unaware of what is taking place and of the gravity of the situation which has been produced.

[1] N. Y. *Times*, July 14, 1949

CHAPTER TWELVE
Where We Stand Today

Thus far I have tried to make clear the proposition that our American system is being destroyed not merely by Communist conspirators, but by all those groups united in the design of luring this country into a Socialist system on the British model. The Communist would like to ruin the American system by clubbing it over the head. The Socialist Planner would like to do it by slow poison. Both types of assassin are at work on it now. For the moment we have limited a little the energies of the assassin with the club. But we must not make the mistake of taking to our bosom the assassin with the poison bottle. Russian communism is merely a more extreme form of socialism than British Fabianism. Russian communism is the grand terminal. British Fabianism is merely a station on the line. The Communist will aid the Planner to get him to that first stop. Those who oppose taking the journey at all must understand the characters and techniques of both groups of schemers.

What I have tried to make clear is that just as the British Socialists operated behind a mask called the Labor Party, so the new-style American Socialist operates behind the mask of Economic Planning.

I have tried to show that in Britain, socialism did not mean State operation of every enterprise. But it did mean socialization of everything—a part through State ownership and the other part, left in private hands, through State planning and control.

The British Socialists moved one step at a time and our American Planners are doing the same thing, always avoiding and even disclaiming the word socialism. The British Socialists used the apparatus of the labor unions and the American Planners have successfully imitated this procedure. The British Fabians moved into the Liberal Party, slowly corrupted it, made it a prisoner because it became utterly dependent on Labor support for success, drove out the orthodox Liberals and ultimately put the Liberal Party out of business, supplanting it with the Labor Party. Here the American Fabians—the Socialist Planners—have moved into the Democratic Party, have made it their helpless tool and are driving out of it the orthodox Democrats. It is merely a question of time when the Democratic Party will go out of business or become absolutely the party of the Planners.

As in England the Fabian Socialists captured the apparatus of great church organizations and infiltrated the organs and instruments of opinion, so the American Planners are performing the same operation here.

We must now ask ourselves how far the Planners have advanced their program for socializing the American society. Having done that, we must then determine what we are to do about it. First, how far has this process of reshaping our political and economic system gone?

I

The depression which began in 1929 produced a deeply questioning mood in the American mind. It seemed to furnish proof that the radical revolutionists were right in their insistence that capitalism was on its last legs. As the depression deepened the mood of frustration grew darker. Meantime, we were being treated to radiant accounts of Russia's five-year plans as distinguished from the planless wilderness of America. By 1933 we moved into the first stage of the Fabian revolution—the Welfare State. The argument ran thus:

Private industry has failed. Its leaders have lost their way. Meantime the jobless starve and lose hope. Therefore the State must step in. This meant actually that the politicians must step into the breach.

We must never lose sight of what the State is. In theory it is the corporate machinery which represents the people in exercising a part of their sovereignty. But the State works through certain machinery and this machinery is operated by politicians. Accordingly, the federal government proceeded to set up a large number of agencies to feed the hungry, to provide work for the unemployed, to round up the youth in CCC camps, to pay money to farmers, set up old-age pension and unemployment systems, to aid students in colleges and so on. The drive for these things was supported by our radical agitators but also by men and women of every type of political philosophy as humane devices to aid the chief victims of the depression.

Thus something almost identical with Lloyd George's aggressive Liberal crusade for all these things, which he began in 1906, got under way here in 1933. We began to hear that the State must provide "jobs for all" and "security for all from the cradle to the grave." And these slogans, without too much examination of all their implications, were sold to the American people. These welfare measures, involving outlays of three or four billion dollars of borrowed money every year, produced a momentary sense of relief. But, despite all the spending, unemployment began to grow again and by 1938 had reached threatening proportions.

The first assumption of the purely political leaders in the government had been that these billions poured into the economic pump would prime it and set business going again. What they overlooked was that the pump was seriously out of repair. This pump was the Capitalist system and it grievously needed fixing. However, during the rise of the Welfare State and the sale of these guarantees of "jobs for all" and "security for all," *nothing whatever was done to repair this pump. On the contrary, much of the government's energy was used in knocking it to pieces and selling to the people the proposition that it was no longer any good, that it had outlived its usefulness.*

Hence in 1938 when the mere social welfare schemes of the government had failed to promote an enduring recovery, we began to hear that something more than mere welfare expenditures was needed. We were then told that the economic system, disorderly and planless, must now be subjected to intelligent and central State planning. Oh, of course, we were not going to scrap the Capitalist system. But we must understand that it must be planned—and planned in the interest of "the people," the "little fellow," the "common man," instead of the big corporations. And this planning must be done under the auspices of the government, which was the agent of the people.

Thus far we followed the history of all western Europe. It began in the early 'seventies of the last century when Bismarck decided to go into competition with the Socialists in establishing the Welfare State. Those who suppose that this American Welfare State which was called the New Deal was something new failed to recognize that it was something quite old.

It originated when the conservatives, first in Germany and then in nearly every continental country, attempted to match the glowing promises of the Socialists. But they realized that the obvious devices of the Welfare State were not sufficient. They had to provide "jobs for all" too. Old-age pensions and doles to widows, orphans, etc., did not provide jobs. The institution that enabled Germany, France, Italy and every continental country to do this was militarism. In Germany it swallowed 600,000 young men from the labor market and created jobs at state expense for three times that many more in the factories and on the farms providing uniforms, shoes, weapons, vehicles, munitions and food for these conscripted armies.

But this cost money, vast sums of money—more than the states could collect by taxes. *And so all of them, year after year, plunged farther and farther into debt* to employ not merely the soldiers but the industrial workers who supplied them and the farms which provided soldiers and horses with food. The end of all this was that nearly every government in continental Europe was buried under insupportable debts by 1914 and was actually on the edge of national bankruptcy. War was a welcome escape.

World War I extricated them from this crisis for four years at least, after which, their economies more gravely disturbed than ever, they all set off upon a more frankly avowed welfare economy plus a Socialist planned economy. We had so-called

Capitalist countries actually operated on the Planned model and managed by statesmen who were Socialists and not interested in making a Capitalist system succeed. World War I had fatally disrupted the Capitalist system in continental Europe. During that war, Walter Rathenau, head of the largest German electrical company, was named to organize the industrial front in Germany. Gradually every German industry was organized under planning bodies with the government as planner. When the war ended Germany had a planned economy. And at this point, Rathenau, the conservative, wrote:

> "From the ruins will arise neither a Communist State nor a system allowing free play to the economic forces. In enterprise the individual will not be given greater latitude; on the other hand individualistic activity will be consciously accorded a part in an economic structure working for Society as a whole; it will be infused with a spirit of communal responsibility and commonweal. *A more equal distribution of possessions and income is a commandment of ethics and economy. Only one in the State is allowed to be immeasurably rich; that is the State itself.*" [1]

This is what post-war Germany tried to do under the Social Democrats—to operate a partially private-enterprise system within a collectivist economy. Indeed this became the model for most of Europe. The idea that the economy must be planned by the State dominated nearly every country. In Germany and Italy, Hitler and Mussolini decided, correctly, as did Stalin in Russia, that this can be done only under a government which possesses the necessary dictatorial powers.

That is what Russia, Italy and Germany were—planned economies. In Russia the decision was for an economy taken over completely by the State and run under State plans. In Italy and Germany the decision was for a system operated partly by the State and partly by private owners under State plans. But in each of these countries they faced the grim fact that this could be done only under a dictatorship. *That is the*

[1] "Social and Economic History of Germany" by Werner Friedrich Bruck, London, 1938. (Italics added.)

only way it can be done. The same thing happened in the Balkan countries and in Greece and Spain where dictatorship, of course, was nothing new. And England is at present confronted with this same stern dilemma.

Now America has been moving deeper and deeper into its imitation of these countries. Already we have discovered that the so-called Welfare State will not make private enterprise work more effectively. Whatever may be said for the Welfare State must be pitched wholly upon the proposition that it is a humane arrangement in which society ought to provide for those unable to provide for themselves. But it will not, of itself, make the economic system work. That is why, by 1938, our American Socialists were able to step into the picture and demand that we plunge further into State action—that we provide not merely welfare but actually take a hand *directly in enterprise and in the planning of the whole economic system.*

Let us see now how far we have proceeded in this seizure of power over the economic system.

Our American Socialist Planners understand, as their British comrades did, the importance to all State action of acquiring a wide control over the whole system of credit. In America we have a central banking system—the Federal Reserve Board and the Federal Reserve Banks. The subject involves technical elements which need not concern us here. It is sufficient to say that originally the Reserve Board was government controlled, but the Reserve Banks were largely dominated by bankers under government regulation.

That has been completely changed. Board and banks are now completely dominated by the government. The power and resources of the banks have been enormously enlarged, so that it may be truthfully said that our government has as large a control over the operations of the private banking system as the socialized Bank of England has over England's banks since the Socialist government took power. It does not yet have the power to decide what types of loans may be made to private industry, but is geared now to assume that power with only a slight alteration in the set-up. It is this which gives the Socialist government of England the power of life and death over every industry in Great Britain.

In 1929 the Reserve Banks had assets of around three billion dollars. They now have assets of 48 billion. At the same time the government has moved into the business of banking, including deposits and money-lending, upon an astonishing scale. The government has a large number of major lending agencies. These are: [2]

The Farm Credit Administration with Land Banks, Banks for Cooperatives, Intermediate Credit Banks, and other lending institutions with loans and investments of	$1,905,000,000
Housing and home financing agencies, including Home Loan Banks, Federal Savings and Loan Associations, Home Owners Loan Corporation, Federal Housing Administration, Public Housing Administration and Federal Deposit Insurance Corporation, all with loans and investments of	1,700,000,000
Reconstruction Finance Corporation, with loans of	1,000,000,000
Export-Import Bank loans of	1,970,000,000

Here is a total of $6,575,000,000. Actually the federal government's direct-banking institutions have outstanding loans greater than the 532 mutual savings banks. They operate 171 offices around the country employing about 27,000 people.

At least as serious is the shape in which the private banking system finds itself. The function of the private banking system is to provide a safe depositary for funds and to make those funds available for investment in building new industries and expanding old ones—creating capital investment. If you will look back at the old bank statements you will find that throughout their history the banks' business was the financing of private enterprise. Today we have about 14,168 private commercial banks.

[2] Task Force Report on Lending Agencies (Appendix R) prepared for Commission on Organization of the Executive Branch of the Government (Hoover Commission), U.S. Gov't Printing Office, 1949.

They are owned by private stockholders and operated by private directors. *But their biggest customer now is the United States government.* By this I mean the largest part of the banks' business is lending money to the United States government. Out of every dollar of the banks' lending business, 30 cents is loaned to private industry, 45 cents to the government and 25 cents is in idle cash. In the mutual savings banks private individuals have loans of six billion dollars, while 14 billion dollars is invested in government loans (bonds).

This is the same sort of evil that has appeared in England in various places. For instance, many manufacturers complain that, with the bulk purchasing system under which the government takes over the entire output of a company for distribution to the people, the government has become their only customer. They are therefore utterly at the mercy of the government and must obey its orders and cultivate its whims or perish. We see this at work in our banks. The government has become the biggest customer of the banks and by its assault upon private enterprise has driven great masses of private borrowers out of the market. I cite this as one of the devices which cunningly subjects a private operator to the power of the government planner.

In the case of some banks and trust companies the private borrower has almost disappeared. In one New York bank and trust company, the deposits are $2,309,000,000. But it holds government bonds and cash to the extent of $1,700,000,000. Another large bank has over 500 million in deposits, over 400 million of which is in U. S. bonds and cash. In another of our very largest banks, for every dollar loaned to individuals, $1.60 is in government obligations. In one smaller New York bank with deposits of 87 million dollars, 85 million is in government obligations.

Why this is so and how it came about is not important at this point. What I am trying to make clear is the extent to which the federal government is moving in on the banking business. All this is the result of government operations in World War I, government operations in welfare and private business in the depression and finally government operations in World War II. One more war and we will, at this rate, see the end of the private banking system, save as a controlled arm of the federal government. And unless we reverse our course we may very well see, even without another war, the end of that sector of the economy. But for the time being the federal power over the national credit agencies on the British model is an accomplished fact.

The most important key economic weapon, next to credit, is electrical power. The public, I think, has little conception of the extent to which our government has penetrated that industry. Up to now the Tennessee Valley Authority (TVA) has been the most ambitious entry into that field, but by no means the only one. The federal government under the Constitution has absolutely no right to engage in the power industry. The action has been made possible by that new group of judges appointed by Franklin D. Roosevelt to the Supreme Court for the specific purpose of repealing or amending the Constitution by judicial decrees.

Our federal government does have authority to engage in flood and navigation control. This has been seized on as the pretext for engaging in the manufacture of electrical power. To control floods and regulate navigation, Congress authorized the TVA to build dams and other installations in navigable rivers. As the dams could be used to produce electrical power the TVA was authorized to produce such power *as was incidental to flood control and navigation.*

Thus the camel got his snout in the tent. The result is that in that valley flood control and navigation are mere incidents and the great project is power. The TVA now has ten steam plants and has just got an initial appropriation to build another huge generating plant—which cannot by any possibility be considered as involved in navigation or flood control.

The TVA has operated at an enormous loss which has been concealed behind tricky bookkeeping. The Government Accounting Office has called attention to this. The whole thing has cost thus far 760 million dollars in investment. But this is only a beginning. The President has sent to Congress a demand for a far more extensive project on the Columbia River which would embrace river systems draining Washington, Oregon, Idaho, and the part of Montana west of the Great Divide.

There are in existence in this region a large group of separate projects, both government and private, all producing more kilowatts than TVA. But President Truman stated in his message that the system might well develop a power potential of 30,-000,000 kilowatts. The size of this can be judged from the fact that TVA is now developing only 2,500,000 kilowatts. And of course this is just the beginning of the program which, if finally concluded, will cover America and take the power industry out of private hands and put it into the hands of the ever-expanding Socialist government.

The Socialist Planners believe they have the private power industry on the run. And they have good reason for believing this. In the last 15 years the government has spent over $3,000,-000,000 on public power projects of various kinds. Compare this with the total fixed assets of the private power companies which are $12,500,000,000.

While the public power systems are to a great degree free of taxes and of interest charges on investment, running countless millions a year, and are permitted bookkeeping practices which would land a private utility official in jail, the private systems are weighed down by every form of government shackles. Private power systems must run at a profit or die. These federal power systems run at losses while proclaiming loudly their fictitious profits.

By 1947 the federal government was generating nine per cent of the total producing capacity of the continental United States. The municipal and state-owned systems were generating 10 per cent, leaving 81 per cent to private industry. But vast expansions of public power are in the works.

The total capacity of the private power systems now is 45,000,000 kilowatts. The present government plans call for government plants generating 41,000,000 kilowatts. Practically all this will be done in the name of reclamation, navigation and flood control. As little as possible will be said about power. And the word socialism will never be used. But the drive is to socialize the power industry of America while at the same time progressively wrecking the private industry by legal and official persecution and official vilification, and by boasting of government financial successes in power operation, as in the case of TVA, which are absolutely false and have been so branded by the Comptroller-general of the United States.

Thus we see the government, under the spur of the Socialist Planners, has been marching through the banks and through the power industry and has ambitious plans for expanding the occupation of these two key services. The men behind these plans are made up of that minority which has now got control of the Democratic Party and its President. He is no more able to resist the demands for all these fantastic enterprises than were the Liberal leaders in England once the Fabian Socialists had that party by the throat. In America the Planners have a force working for them which will be irresistible. It is an old political weapon—pork. The people of the TVA region have enjoyed the spending of $760,000,000 mostly in those five southern states comprising the so-called Tennessee Valley, together with power sold at a low rate, though at a loss.

Now the Columbia River region, covering four western states, wants the same. Of course there are some 16 other plans—great and moderate in size—for other regions. Farm, labor and even business interests in those regions will be expected to get behind the drive, each for its share of the pork. The congressman from one region will be expected to vote for the plans in all the other regions in order to get the support of those regions for his own plans. They will be thinking about the lush pickings for their respective regions in these floods of federal money. They will not be thinking about the total result of all this, which will be the ultimate delivery of our society into the Socialist column. Yet that is the issue.

Do we want a Socialist society or not? The movements for these plans go on, but never do the advocates use the word socialism. What we hear about is power for the farmer, credit for the farmer and the "little fellow," power for your state and my state, business for the cement man and the steel man and the building industry, houses for all, floods of money for everything, jobs for all, security for all, a society planned and running smoothly on a program emerging from the "Brain" in Washington, money for the farmers, jobs for the workers, something for everybody. No one thing is called socialism. But when it is all put together the completed structure will be a Socialist state. One recalls the workman in Hitler's factory for making baby carriages, where each employee secretly worked on only one part, but when one workman whose wife was expecting a baby decided to take home stealthily one of each part and put them together, what he got was not a baby carriage but a machine gun.

Another project now under heavy pressure by the Socialist Planners is socialized medicine. It is, of course, not called socialized medicine, but health insurance. The plan came, ostensibly, out of the Federal Security Agency from Mr. Oscar R. Ewing, its head. It calls for an increase, with federal aid, of the number of hospitals, doctors and nurses and dentists, along with what he calls compulsory health insurance. This is a plan similar to the one now operating in Britain under its Socialist government. Under it all employers and their employees would be taxed at the payroll window, as in the case of old-age pensions and unemployment insurance, for medical care. The proponents of this scheme had the effrontery to call it "free medical care." Of course it is not. It will be paid for by taxes which will come out of everyone's pocket. This would mean, of course, that, as in England, the patient would choose his doctor, but the doctors would be paid by the government and would be under its general management. The system is now on trial in England. It is by every standard of judgment a ghastly failure.

What the American must understand, however, is that while each of these proposals—federal invasion of banking, federal invasion of power and socialized medicine—is promoted as if it were just a single reform unrelated to all the others, the simple fact is that *each is intended to liquidate some sector of the private enterprise system and expand the area of socialism.* When the whole program is well advanced, we will be a socialized people upon the British model.

What about the railroads and the mines? This problem the Planners feel will almost solve itself. There is no point in agitating for it now. The country is not ready. They know, despite what they say publicly, that sooner or later the country must face a critical economic condition. This is the moment for which they wait. It must be remembered that at least three times in the last 30 years the government has taken over the railroads. It operated them for 18 months during the first World War at a cost to the taxpayers of $1,123,500,000. It took over several barge canals and their equipment at that time and did not return these to private owners until 1924.

After World War II, on May 17, 1946, the President ordered the head of the Office of Defense Transportation to seize the railroads, which he did, holding them until May 26th, when the strike was settled. And again in 1948 the President ordered the Secretary of the Army to take the roads. He held them for several months.

This has happened, and in the event of a strike in a serious depression it could happen again. And the government might never give them back, a course which would not be difficult if the roads and their stockholders, as well might be, were threatened with bankruptcy and did not want them back. During the depression years, before World War II, the chairman of the board of one railroad actually tried to start an agitation for the government to take over the railroads. It seemed then the only chance of saving the bondholders.

However, our over-eager Planners are not trusting wholly to time. Already an assault upon the railroads has begun. The Department of Justice has charged that the roads collected unreasonable freight rates from the government during the war. The Department wants to recover these for the government. These charges are estimated to be not less than $2,000,000,000, three times the working capital of the railroads. The road officials insist that the maximum charge to the government was never more than to private shippers and on great quantities of freight it was substantially less. Of course if the government obtained such a judgment against the railroads they would never be able to pay it. If the government foreclosed no one would buy them save the government, which it could do without putting up a cent—simply using the judgment to pay the bill.

The railroad spokesmen have charged that this is a deliberate attempt to wreck the financial structure of the roads and to hasten the day of government ownership and control. The obvious injustice of the whole project, however, is evident when we realize that the government has already collected in taxes on profits most of any excess charges which the roads may have charged, assuming that they did so.

As for the mines, the government has taken them over more than once during strikes, just as it has done in the case of the railroads. This it did when the mines were enjoying war prosperity. It might take them during a strike in a period of depression—and never return them.

And what of steel? What indeed! Has not the President of the United States already announced his wish to have authority from Congress to build additional steel mills because he believed the private steel industry was not producing enough steel? He was being egged on to this by his Socialist labor-leader supporters who are eagerly searching for the weak point at which the government can get started on this course.

So much for direct government operation. As to government planning of the privately owned sector of the economy, we do not have to speculate any more. The plans have now been made public fully enough. When I began to write this small volume I had set out in my notes my expectations as to what would be attempted in this field. I had no notion, at that point, that so daring a proposal would be made as has now been bared in Washington. Had I forecast such a proposal a few months ago I would have been branded as a deranged alarmist. Now that the plans have been made public they turn out to be far worse than anything I anticipated.

The American people cannot afford to be in any doubt about

these plans. They spell the end of our long history of private property and the definite entrance of this country into a State-Planned Socialist system upon a scale almost as far as Britain had traveled two years ago. If, by some chance, these plans which I am now about to describe go through, the rest will follow swiftly. And we can write finis to the American free society.

This will be a grave misfortune for Americans. It will be a disaster of the first magnitude for the rest of the world. It is extremely doubtful that these plans can be forced through now. The real significance of them is that they reveal the distance to which these Socialist Planners, backed by the President of the United States, are prepared now to go.

II

Perhaps no experiment among all the strange enterprises of the last 18 years came to such a complete and inglorious end as the NRA. When the Supreme Court killed it even its heartiest supporters were relieved. And the President himself told Miss Frances Perkins it was just as well because "it was just a head-ache." What can one say now as one reads the plans that have been laid before Congress for the revival of something infinitely more fantastic than the NRA, plans which can be described as nothing less than weird?

One of these proposals relates chiefly to industry and is known as the Spence Act. The other relates to the farm and is known as the Brannan Plan. Spence is a New Deal congressman from Kentucky and Brannan is Secretary of Agriculture. But actually both plans originated with the Socialist Planners around Mr. Brannan and they represent the federal administration's approach to the Planned Economy.

The Spence Act [3] declares that its purpose is to fulfill the government's responsibility to "promote maximum employment, production and purchasing power." Of course this is a

[3] H.R. 2756, introduced Feb. 15, 1949.

worthy objective but it is made the excuse for literally taking over the economic system by the government.

The proposed act gives the government vast powers which it can use under certain conditions. These conditions are:

1. When there is a shortage of materials or facilities which injures "free enterprise" or which causes high prices or gets in the way of our foreign policy, our national security or our economic growth.

2. When price increases tend to unbalance the economy or .mpede employment opportunities or adversely affect business conditions, etc.

These conditions are stated in such broad terms that the President can use them whenever it suits his purposes, and under the plan he is to be the *sole judge* whether or not the conditions exist.

If this act becomes law here is what the President can do:

1. He can decide how much ought to be produced of any essential commodity—steel, coal, grains, lumber, anything. He can make up a national production budget *which industry will be directed to meet under government plans and compulsions.*

2. He can decide it should be done by private enterprise, in which case he can "promote consultation between business, labor, farmers and the government." And he may then decide on programs to "supplement private enterprise." The President can compel management and labor to sit down with the State on the Reuther plan and make plans for a whole industry. This can be organized as a continuing operation. Furthermore it does not have any of the protective limitations of the old NRA.

3. The President can contract with the laboratories of private industry to engage in specified research projects and provide funds to do so under his direction. When a new discovery or invention or process is perfected in this way he can patent it in the name of the government and throw it open to public use under government license. This brings into existence the Planners' dream of government control of research and its fruits.

4. He may purchase here or abroad any materials he deems necessary.

5. He may make loans to industry, states or cities to expand their capacity to produce materials or perform services.

6. If the President decides private industry cannot or will not expand its capacity he may construct new plants, factories, mines, anything he deems necessary. And he may enter into contracts with private persons to operate these government-owned facilities or he may create government-owned corporations to do so. Here is the authority, for instance, for the government to go into the steel business—which the President recently demanded. With this law he could, without consulting Congress, go into the steel, copper, aluminum, coal, agricultural machinery, chemical or any other business he believed necessary "to improve our economic condition."

7. He may establish voluntary priorities for materials after consultation with industry and if this doesn't work he may set up compulsory priorities and allocations of materials. Which means that to buy any material—if the President so ordains—the private manufacturer must first get permission from the President, who will decide in what order and in what quantity he will get it. *Here is the power of life and death over every industrial enterprise in the land*

8. He is authorized to regulate imports and exports as was done during the war. This is the power which Hitler possessed, as he possessed all the others granted in this act—those powers which enabled him truly to be called a dictator.

9. No private business concern can raise a price without giving the President up to 60 days' notice and he can then refuse it permission to do so.

10. He may establish maximum prices on materials or facilities if he believes them necessary. *Here is the beginning of the end of the price system without which the private-enterprise economy cannot possibly exist.*

To carry out these amazing powers, which will make the President, in time of peace, the czar of American enterprise, he may lay down such rules as he may deem necessary to carry out the provisions of the Spence Act. This sets him up as a law-maker. And he may "make such inspection of the books, records and other writings, premises or property of any person and make such investigations and conduct such hearings as may be necessary or appropriate to the enforcement or administration of this act."

Here is the power of seizure and search upon a hitherto unimaginable scale.

This is the Planned Economy so far as industry is concerned, almost precisely as England now has it and which the British Fabian believes to be an essential part of his socialism. It provides for the government's entry into production as an enterpriser, and for complete government planning of the privately owned sector of our economy. President Truman recently assured us that he was for a "planned economy," but he was not for a "controlled" economy. Of course there can be no Planned Economy without controls.

If this law were enacted this country would be further along the road to the Socialist Planned Economy than England was three years ago. This is not an emergency measure. It is a five-year plan. It is not something to be set up to get us out of a present hole. It is the application of the principle of State planning to our economy. But, in essence, it is not a plan at all. It is merely a measure to constitute the President of the United States the Supreme Planner—with the power to make a plan and more plans and to do anything he believes necessary to carry out those plans. It is important to call attention to the very essential fact that it is not a plan. One of the curious features about the British Fabians was that when they took office they discerned they had been talking about "planning," when as a matter of fact they had merely been talking about *getting the power to plan*. And when they got the power *they had no plans*, and had to confess as much.

What appears in this Spence Act, of course, is only one part of the scheme. There is also the Brannan Plan, embodied in Senate bills 1971 and 1882, which will apply to agriculture. While the President's attempt to rush this Act through Congress failed, it reveals the government's designs and the kind of world into which we are being pushed.

Up to now the government has been pegging prices to provide high prices for farmers. But the harassed housewife has been crying out in anguish against these prices. To meet this situation—and make everybody happy—the government has invented an incredible scheme. There will be no more government pegging of farm prices. The farmer will sell his produce in the open market at whatever prices he can get. This will give the housewife the benefit of a low price. That takes care of her—so she may think.

The other prong of the scheme is to give the farmer his same old high prices. A price level for produce will be fixed. Then the government will pay the farmer the difference between the price at which he sells his crop and the price which the government guarantees. For instance, if the guaranteed price on his crop were fixed at $2000 and it brought in the open market only $1500, the government would pay him the remaining $500.

This money would, of course, come out of taxes, and the consumer who might be lulled into thinking he was getting a lower price would, it is hoped, not realize that he was paying the difference in taxes. To put it differently, the farmer would be paid for his crop by two persons—one part by the consumer and the other part by the government. But of course the consumer would really pay it all, save that one part he would pay indirectly to the farmer through the government in taxes, with the additional charge of the salaries of bureaucrats needed to run this show.

There are 5,800,000 farmers. The plan will apply to wheat, corn, cotton, tobacco, milk, hogs, eggs, chickens, beef cattle, lamb, fruits and vegetables. Now who is going to check on these millions of farmers to determine the price at which each sold his crop, to ascertain how much was still due by the government? There would have to be questionnaires, regional offices, local offices and an army of bureaucrats. No one has yet calculated the cost of this, which would come out of taxes and would be one more hidden item in the cost of our foods. This is the plan now in effect in Britain which Sir Stafford Cripps has declared is so great a strain on the government that it must be curtailed.

However, there is a joker in the plan, designed to put the big farmer, the most successful farmer, out of business and to liquidate anybody who does not sign up with the plan. The general idea is to give its benefits only to the small farmer. It is therefore limited to farmers who raise only 1800 units. Now what is a unit? Well, a unit of corn would be 10 bushels. If he raised nothing but corn he could raise only 1800 units, which would be 18,000 bushels. If he complied he could sell his corn for whatever he could get and collect the balance from the government to make up the guaranteed price. The law would fix the size of a unit as applied to all other crops. A man might raise corn, lambs, chickens, milk, fruit and vegetables. He would have to keep the total of all within the limit of 1800 units. If he exceeded these 1800 units he would be out, and would have to be satisfied with the market price.

But who is going to check up on all these farmers to determine whether or not each keeps within his 1800 units? Here is to be another army of bureaucrats and more mountains of questionnaires and reports. Even so radical a farm champion as Senator Aiken, who can generally swallow a pretty big dose, backs away from this. He told reporters that such a program cannot stop at the farm. If the government undertakes to guarantee a satisfactory income to the farmer, can we deny the same guarantee to other income groups?

Obviously it cannot stop at the farm. The government cannot step into the economic system and monkey with prices and wages and income of one group of producers without setting in motion innumerable forces in other groups. And no man can tell where it will end, to say nothing of the inconceivable antics that will take place in the inevitable black markets. Secretary Brannan has thus far refused to estimate the cost, but others have indicated it might run from *five to ten billion dollars a year in additional taxes.*

Where will these additional taxes come from? They will come out of that part of the producing world which provides our industrial materials. For the ten billion must be paid by someone. That ten billion dollars, therefore, must inevitably show up in the higher prices of non-farm goods. And it will have two inevitable results. One will be that the higher prices for industrial products will result in a decreased demand for them. The other will be that higher taxes will kill the profits of the smaller and least efficient industrial units. The liquidation of these units is always the inevitable consequence of plans to make one sector of the business world pay part of the bills or profits of another.

Thus we may form a picture of the society into which we are being tempted by the bait of government planning and spending. These are not schemes which may at some distant day appear as a program of government. *They are the program of the present government and have been announced as such.*

From it all emerges the spectacle of a society in which the government makes itself responsible for the security of every citizen from the cradle to the grave and for the continuous operation of the entire machinery of business and farming. The ultimate aim is to control banks, transportation, power, mines and the basic metal industries and, I am quite sure, the entire business of life insurance, fire insurance and other forms of insurance. The rest of the industrial system will be operated by private owners but under plans to be made by the President under broad powers and through a multitude of planning and enforcement bureaus. The farms will be brought under the wing of the government through production quotas, subsidies, allocations and priorities.

This corresponds in every essential respect to the system now in operation in England. And this is what we will have here if the men now in power in our government are permitted to have their way.

Of course there is no provision for the peace-time conscription of labor, as in Britain. There was no provision for this in Britain when the great proletarian dream was being pictured in bright colors before the eyes of English working men. But the Socialists got around to it. The power to compel the British workman to move from one job to another and even to go far from his home is now in the hands of the Ministry. And, of course, so it will be here. There is no alternative. *This kind of planning is futile unless the power to compel all—employer and employee alike—to conform to the plans can be used.*

This, then, is the road we are traveling. It is the road to socialism. And we will continue to travel it until the masses of Americans who still cherish the tradition of a free society understand where they are traveling, and take vigorous measures first to halt the journey and then to reverse it.

CHAPTER THIRTEEN
What To Do

WE MUST now ask: What can be done?

One of the first things those opposed to this socialistic program must do is to rid themselves of the moral intimidation which has been imposed on their minds. In the debate around this problem, the American system has been painted as something wicked, bungling, even brutal, while the Planned New World of the future will be filled with sweetness, light and plenty. The very word "profit" has been endowed with the most sinister implications. When our new Planned Paradise is opened for business the very nature of men will be altered. If you oppose these plans it is, of course, because you are sitting upon some immoral concession of the profit system from which you do not wish to be dislodged.

In the morning paper on the day I write this the President scolds the opposition to socialized medicine (which he calls "health insurance") because it represents nothing but the selfish interest of "organized medicine" fighting to preserve its "exclusive monopoly." Whatever may be said of the 180,000 doctors in this country, certainly they cannot be called monopolists. And is it not barely possible that there may be something more than a mere selfish interest in the opposition to socialized medicine, even among the doctors?

If we speak against government-owned power, it is immediately resolved into a "battle" between the "people" (or even the "little people") and the "greedy power barons." But is there not another interest involved here? No one knows better than I do that there are grave maladjustments in our economic system, and that there are those who get less of the world's bounty than people should have. Is it not a question as to how the best results can be obtained for our people as a whole? Is this to be achieved in a private or a Socialist economy?

It is not a choice between a perfect system called socialism and an imperfect system called capitalism. It is a choice between two human systems both of which will inevitably have their imperfections because they are human. But the Socialist Planners do not concede this. Capitalism they present to us only in terms of its defects. But socialism is painted only in terms of the wonderful things it is going to do some day.

But we do not have to rely on the promises any longer. Socialism in various forms has had plenty of trial. Russia is a Socialist country though the Socialists would like to escape that fact. The old Socialists who first lifted the torch in Russia talked of the perfect day of the free life which they would bring. No one arraigned tyranny more vigorously than Lenin. But when they set their ideal into motion it rushed along to its inevitable end—tyranny, the most terrible tyranny in history.

The old Socialists, with their luminous dreams, got power in Germany after World War I, and operated a society not greatly different from that now in effect in England—partially nationalized and partially planned. It ended in fascism and Hitler, for the line between fascism and Fabian socialism is very thin. Fabian socialism is the dream. Fascism is Fabian socialism plus the inevitable dictator.

In Italy, Socialists of various schools dominated the political life of that nation with the same results as in Germany, and that too ended in fascism and Mussolini.

Now England makes the experiment, blown up with promises of freedom. But already she has got around to the ways of the tyrant. She asserts over the worker the right to say where he shall or shall not work. She asserts the right to throw the farmer who does not meet her directives off his farm. And this English experiment would collapse tomorrow if the strong arm of American capitalism were withdrawn from its support. Indeed it is collapsing now even with that powerful arm around it.

On the other hand, the greatest and most efficient producing machine in the world is in this country. This did not happen by accident. It is the result of the soil of freedom in which it grew. Indeed to my mind the great, decisive factor in the choice between socialism and capitalism is that the system of production by private enterprise in a severely restrained republican government is the only one in which men can enjoy the inestimable blessing of freedom. Socialism is impossible under any condition, but if it can be made to work at all it must be under an all-powerful State with the vast powers necessary to enforce its decrees governing every sector of our lives.

There are none of these reforms now so earnestly desired which cannot be obtained in far greater measure in a free society under private enterprise. After all the rosy promises from the State, old-age pensions give such a pittance that labor is now turning back to private industry to provide adequate retirement funds by private agreement. Unemployment insurance is now provided under state laws. The only thing the federal government does is to collect the taxes and literally steal nearly a billion dollars a year out of them for other purposes than unemployment insurance.

As for socialized medicine, what is desired? Today in America we have the most widely applied medical service and the most extensive hospitalization ever attained anywhere. Under the new voluntary insurance plans such as the famous "Blue Cross" plan, this private service has been enormously extended to millions of people who could not afford it before. For the lowest income groups there is the free service of the clinics, both municipal and private.

There remains a part of the population still not receiving adequate medical care because it is too poor or because it is scattered in thinly populated areas far from doctors or hospitals. What is the obvious course for intelligent people? Is it not to hold what we have and then seek to extend its benefits to still greater numbers, rather than to destroy the fine care now given the immense majority of our people and reduce the whole population to the level of the poorest group? Beyond doubt the least adequate part of our service is that given in the free clinics because of the great number to be serviced.

Socialized medicine, we now know from Britain's experience, will ruin what we have and reduce the whole nation to the level of the service now provided in the free clinics.

What of houses? Building houses for the lowest income group in the nation is now impossible because of two things: (1) The appalling taxes which show up in the price of everything and which account for at least 25 per cent of the cost of every house. (2) The restrictions on output and on the use of modern methods of production which organized labor imposes on the housing industry. The principal victims of this are the workers themselves.

Of one thing I am certain (and I can speak out of a long and wide experience) and that is that we will never get adequate housing out of government building. It has been attempted over and over again and always with the most glaring and pathetic failure. The way to get houses is to release the energies of the private-enterprise system. Indeed the way to get whatever we require is to take the government off the backs of the great productive instrumentalities of the nation.

As for the labor unions, there is no right or privilege they want or are entitled to which they cannot have in a system of private enterprise. There is nothing more certain than that the Socialist State, wherever it is tried, will ultimately get around to liquidating the power of the labor unions. The first warning to the British Socialist government to slow up on nationalization came from the Trades Union Council. The next came from the cooperatives. These were the two most powerful economic units in the movement to bring socialism to England.

I suggest that the road we are traveling is sufficiently clear. We cannot delude ourselves with the expectation that we may go a little way further and then stop in the belief that we can combine socialism and capitalism and preserve the best features of each. The very first hard and cold fact we must face is that *these two systems cannot live together in the same society*, despite the spurious claims for the so-called mixed system in some of the Scandinavian countries which has never been submitted to any test.

If we keep on the way we are going, nothing can save the Capitalist sector from extinction. Why? Because it will be called upon inevitably to pay the cost of operating its own sector and the greater portion, if not all, of the cost of operating the Socialist sector.

In the United States the government-operated industries we have, though few, are operated at a loss. *The private industries must produce the income out of which the losses of these government industries are paid and all the costs of government as well.* The broader the publicly operated sector, the narrower will be the private sector, while the load it must support in taxes will be increased.

We are on the road to socialism and we will continue on that road to the final consummation of this wrong-headed dream unless we make a conscious and robust effort to halt it.

As I write these lines, the nation is sliding toward the inevitable crisis. Its follies and extravagances are overtaking it. This crisis will be our great hour of decision. It is at this point we must arrest the course of the social disease that is destroying us and set our hands to the hard task of lifting up and revivifying our shattered system of free enterprise. If we do not rise equal to this decision in this fateful hour, the power to save our great heritage of freedom will have passed out of our hands and we will go on stumbling down the path along which Europe has slipped under the same forces that are destroying us.

It is not, of course, possible here to lay down a program in detail for checking and reversing our direction. And it is not necessary. What is necessary is to have the broad outlines of the shape such a program ought to take, to see clearly the general principles which must govern the effort. These I will now attempt to set out as briefly as possible.

I

We must put HUMAN FREEDOM once again as the first of our demands. There can be no security in a nation without freedom.

Freedom must have first place in our loyalties—and then economic security. Never in history has so much been spoken and sung about human freedom as a motive of sacrifices as in the last ten years. Never has so little attention been given to the element of human freedom by those who have been declaiming and singing about it. We were exhorted to throw away the lives of our youth, to load the coming generations with debt, to pour out mountains of our wealth—for what? To save the mere fragments and shadows of freedom that still survived in western Europe. But when we talk about freedom as the vital element in our own society, we are met with the sneer: Freedom for what? Freedom to starve?

Is it possible that the sneerers mean by this that they would imperil or even throw away the freedom of a whole people to improve the economic condition of a part? There must be some better way to do it. Let us work to make our country a more bountiful home for all to live in. But the first and indispensable test of every plan for this must be—will it impair our freedom? A better life for all, yes—but not at the expense of our liberties.

II

We must stop apologizing for our Capitalist society.

It has made us strong without corrupting our humane sympathies for the world of starving or staggering collectivist and semi-collectivist nations around us. When you hear the sneers of critics from across the waters, remember that they come from people who are crying to us for help and who are sneering at the social system that made us strong enough to give it. We have been a good neighbor in the family of nations, most of which are bowed or wholly prostrate under the wreckage of their collectivist experiments. Second to our love of freedom must come our resolve to *stand up for the American way.*

III

Not one more step into socialism. Hold the line for the American way of life.

This is imperative. We have been led along step by step. In our ignorance and folly and confusion we have yielded at each step. At some point along this course we will make the final critical surrender which will make reversal of the course impossible. We will go so far that we will lose the power of decision over our fate and the final march to full socialism will become inevitable. There is, of course, much to be done to repair all the damage to our system. But the first militant maneuver in our grand strategy must be our determination, taken at once, to *hold the line* for the *American way here*. We must stand resolutely against one more step. *Not one more step toward socialism. Not one more surrender. Not one more compromise. Let us hold the line where we stand.*

IV

Get rid of the compromising leaders.

To this end let us put a mark upon every man in public life who is willing to surrender further. The one most destructive feature in the defense of America against these alien isms has been the politician who is more interested in election than in principle and who has been foolish enough and weak enough to convince himself that the best defense against further Socialist progress was to surrender at each stage of the battle. Let there be an end of the weak and compromising leaders.

V

We must recognize that we are in the midst of a revolution—that it is war—and that we must begin to fight it as such.

We are in a war—a social war—and we must understand that character of it. Our enemies have ruthlessly and, in places, savagely, carried on a campaign to get possession of all the instruments of opinion and information. They have not captured all of them. But while one large section of our schools and press have attended to their proper function of educating our youth and of printing the news fairly and freely, these revolutionary forces have managed to lay hold of many of the instrumentalities of the classroom, the platform, the pulpit, the movies and the radio upon an amazing scale and to use them, not for their legitimate purposes of education, information and entertainment, but to carry on a concerted attack upon the minds of the American people, to mold the opinions of readers and audiences and to drive from the press, the air, the movies and the bookshops, by organized boycotts and organized smearing, all who have dared to stand up for our American way of life. This challenge must be accepted boldly, resolutely and militantly. We must launch a broad, vigorous campaign to educate our electorate on the true nature of the grave crisis which menaces our civilization.

VI

We must put an end to the orgy of spending that is rapidly bankrupting the nation.

Among the most critical conditions that menace us are the fantastic commitments for spending unimaginable billions and the crushing weight of our national debt upon our economic system. What we shall do about this debt is one of the great problems we shall have to deal with as soon as we set about a full-scale program of rehabilitation of our sadly disarranged national household. Its full weight we have not yet felt. There is not the slightest doubt that the recent war cost at least A HUNDRED BILLION DOLLARS more than it should have cost because of the appalling inefficiency and the wild, unreasoning extravagance of men who had lost touch with reality as they played with these unaccustomed billions.

But what can we say of the record since the war in Europe ended in May, 1945? *From July 1, 1945 to June 30, 1949—Mr. Truman's years in power—he will have spent 184 billion dollars. This is 30 billion dollars more than was spent by this government in the 147 years of its existence from Washington up to the end of Roosevelt's first administration.*

When is this to end? We must therefore decide at once that we will not permit one more cent for any purpose beyond our present commitments.

VII

We must put an end to crisis government in America.

Since 1940 this nation has been living on war. It has been the excuse for spending fabulous billions and filling every man's pocket with a share in the black profits of war. From 1940 to 1945 we borrowed and spent billions in a shooting war. Since 1945—nearly five years—we have been spending billions in what we are told is a "cold war." Unless we make an end of this it will bankrupt us. Even more appalling, it will lead us into another war at the end of which our liberties and our economic system will be ready for the scrap heap. The reason for all this is that the interests of America have been completely blotted out in this insane adventure in world salvation. We have saved nothing. We are contributing to the destruction of everything our civilization values. We are being led along by noisy minorities and eager revolutionaries who use the world crisis to destroy our way of life or whose interests are in other lands, and by bungling politicians dependent upon crisis as an institution to remain in power. The time is here for all those who believe in America and who want above all to save *her* to stand up and make their voices heard above the clamor of the minorities who are destroying us.

VIII

We must stop "planning" for socialism and begin planning to make our free system of private enterprise operate at its highest capacity.

No one can object to planning if the word is used in its normal dictionary sense. It is the cunning use of the word planning as a synonym for socialism to which we object. It comes down to this: Whether we are for making plans to destroy our system and substituting British Fabian socialism, or for making plans to enable the system of private production to work and to save the American way of life.

The Capitalist system can operate at its fullest efficiency only when there is a full and free flow of savings into investment—

the creation of new capital machinery or the expansion of old. Whatever encourages that stimulates the system. Whatever hampers or checks that slows it down and ultimately destroys it.

Since 1933, the government has waged relentless war upon this system, in the first years ignorantly but in its final phases with a definite design to cripple and destroy it. This must come to an end. What this nation needs above all is men and women who are willing to create jobs. A job is an opportunity to work at a task producing useful wealth or useful services. Every man who starts a little shop to provide work for himself benefits the system. If he provides work for himself and one other he doubles his useful contribution to the system's energy. If he can make enough profit to save and expand his business to employ ten and then a hundred and then a thousand he is the most useful type of citizen we have.

Yet he has been pilloried as our greatest criminal and the government has taken every conceivable measure to prevent him from accumulating those savings which alone make expansion possible. It has held him up to public scorn and hatred. It has taxed away his savings and it has so choked the streams through which savings flow into investment that our system is now wilting away before our very eyes. It is a fact that today despite the addition of 20 million to our population, the number of people employed in private enterprise upon the business of producing goods and services for the people directly is actually smaller than it was 20 years ago. The rest owe their jobs to government directly or to the production of war materials or other products for the government.

Therefore our course must be to stop planning for socialism and begin planning to encourage and revive free private enterprise. There are many defects to be cured—old imperfections and far more destructive new ones. Our system is in an appalling mess now, what with the debt, the confiscatory taxes which draw the blood from its very veins, government intrusions and the threats of ultimate extinction that are taking ever more terrifying shape. The task will call for patriotism and courage. But it must not be delayed another day.

IX

We must set about rebuilding in its integrity our republican system of government.

The present regime in our federal government has declared war upon our Constitution and has found the means of by-passing its provisions and almost completely changing our whole political system. It may be that we can never recapture all of our old and sound institutions. But we can recapture most of them.

We must understand these institutions; we must realize the terrible work of destruction our revolutionary Planners have done upon them. We must begin to return government to the states. We must curb the grasping hand of the federal government. We must restrain the grasping hand of the Executive. And our very first step must be to make a list of the emergency powers granted to the Executive for war purposes and then repeal every one of them.

X

We cannot depend on any political party to save us. We must build a power outside the parties so strong that the parties will be compelled to yield to its demands.

We must realize that this battle is now being lost because our leaders have understood nothing of the terrible weapon of modern European revolutionary propaganda. They have made the mistake of supposing the battle could be left to congressmen and senators and political leaders, that they could distribute literature telling of the wonders of capitalism and then leave the whole battle to be fought out in elections. Then when the elections have come around they have discovered that their own candidates were not more than 50 per cent on their side.

Business leaders raise a million dollars to advertise, like a new breakfast food, the "wonders of capitalism." You never hear our Planners advertising the wonders of socialism. Yet they are taking over the country. They understand that people are dominated extensively by personal and group interests, that this is a natural phenomenon and that the personal and group interests at any given moment exercise a more immediate and potent stimulation upon their thinking than broad ideological principles. The Communists and their intermittent allies, the Socialist Planners, have carried on their propaganda inside the schools and colleges, the churches, the press, radio and movies, inside labor unions and even trade associations and professional groups, inside racial, religious and cultural groups in this war upon the American mind.

Conservatives have looked with amazement and frustration at the surrenders made by the leaders in both the Republican and Democratic parties. They should have learned by now that this powerful weapon of radical revolutionary propaganda has been far more influential in their party conventions than the speeches of their party leaders. When the issue of federal seizure of electric power arises, the utility companies charge to the defense. We then behold a battle between the "money-grasping" utility magnates and the "unselfish" hosts of the Brave New World. After this battle the utility warriors retreat to their barracks to lick their wounds.

Presently another battle begins. This time it is over the proposal to socialize medicine. Now it takes on the appearance of a struggle between "the selfish agents of the organized medical monopoly" and the men whose hearts are bleeding for the wretched men and women who are suffering and dying like flies for want of a pill to alleviate their sufferings. This is a fight for the doctors and off they go to the battle alone, as ignorant as children of the force they are fighting, amateur recruits without weapons or plans against trained leaders in a brand new school of social warfare.

And so it goes. What we must get into our minds is that this is not a succession of unrelated battles against doctors or utility magnates or steel barons. *It is one big war against our civilization.* And the sooner we realize this—that every battle is everybody's battle, that every battle must be fought by the combined forces of all and that leadership must pass into the hands of men who understand this new kind of warfare—the sooner we will begin to check the forces of the enemy.

There was some excuse for the failure of the British to stem this tide. First, their system had been appallingly injured by World War I. Second, it had been more desperately wrecked by World War II—by the war effort itself and by the disintegration of their colonial empire and their foreign markets. But more than this, the British Conservatives and Liberals were facing a form of civil and economic warfare from within, which they did not understand because it was new.

But there is no such excuse for us. We have the spectacle of Britain before us. Moreover, badly as we have been hurt by our depression and by World War II and by the still more damaging distortions of our system by the Socialist Planners and their innocent allies, nevertheless the great fundamental elements of strength are still here and we have the benefit of the English experience as a lesson to guide us.

We must now go back to fundamentals. Our fathers gave to the world the sublime example of statesmen who had found the means of casting off the tyrant State and building up the sovereign people—unleashing the energies of free men. It was this historic experiment which set off that astonishing surge of human energy which created here such abundance—and such freedom—as the world has never known.

Now in the last 16 years a new set of enemies, drawing their inspiration from the crumbling ruins of European societies, have been busy rebuilding the power of the all-powerful State and constricting the freedoms of the people. They believe, and with some reason, that if they can carry forward this objective a little further, they will have definitely reversed the course of history beyond our power to alter it.

The task before us is clear. For our principles of action we must go back to our Constitution, to our Declaration of Independence, to our history and to the example set by our national fathers.

We must begin now to dismantle the tyrant State in America and to build up once again the energies of a free people.